Cemeteries

of

West Providence Township, Bedford County, Pennsylvania

Michele L. Miller

ISBN: 1986127419
ISBN-13: 978-1986127417

Thank you to the following people who provided me with information for this book:
Susan Calhoun
Niels Witkamp
Ron McFarland
Bob Felton
Carolyn Carroll
Bronwyn Graham
Angie Price
Bedford County Historical Society

Thanks to everyone who so kindly and willingly gave me information, those that took time out of their busy day to help me, the property owners who graciously allowed me to cross their property. I sincerely appreciate the time you spent with me and I am very fortunate! Your support and assistance has been invaluable throughout this journey. You have all been so kind and helpful. I sincerely apologize if I forgot to mention anyone who helped make this publication a success!

In a work of this kind it is quite unavoidable that there shall be some omissions and some error of statement. A great deal of care and effort was put forth as each cemetery was inventoried and recorded. I exercised as much caution as possible to accurately record all gravestone data and information.

While every effort was made to ensure the most accuracy of the GPS Coordinates, it is always best to double check your route and refer to a map before beginning your drive.

I am sure there are a few mistakes that might exist with this volume of information. If any errors are detected, I certainly apologize to the family. However, please contact me as soon as possible so that corrections may be made. If you have verifiable knowledge and proof that a person is buried in a particular cemetery and the grave is unmarked, please send me that information as well and I will include it in future reprints.

Please note:

I have walked through and documented every cemetery in this book. I took photos of each stone and made notes of the inscriptions. I spent several months documenting these cemeteries to the best of my ability. Notes have been made throughout this book with credit given to anyone that has helped me along the way and also to anyone's work that I have referenced.

Each Veteran is noted with a  in the Misc. Info column of the Cemetery Listing.

For more information please visit:

www.southamptontownshipbooks.com

Table of Contents

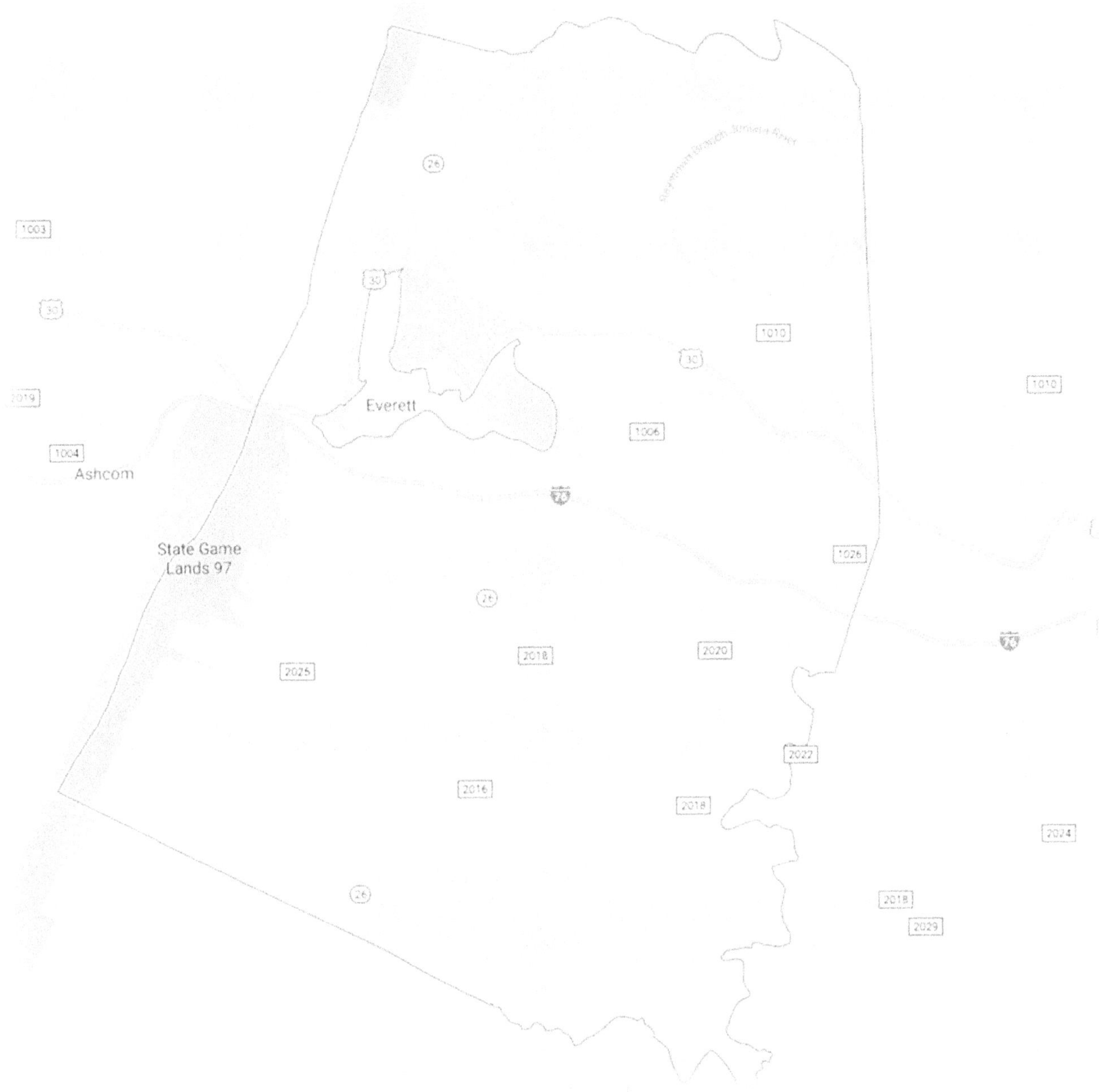

Outline of West Providence Township
(Everett Borough is outlined inside West Providence)
Please note Everett Cemetery is not included in this book because it is inside of Everett Borough.
Image from Google Maps

West Providence Township Cemeteries Map Key			
1	Baughman Union Church Cemetery	11	McDaniel Farm Cemetery
2	Bussard Cemetery (Warrior Ridge)	12	Morgart and Morgret Cemetery
3	Calhoun Farm Cemetery	13	Mount Union Christian Church Cemetery
4	Cherry Lane Church Cemetery	14	O'Neal Farm Cemetery
5	Clark Farm Cemetery	15	Ritchey Farm Cemetery
6	Dibert Farm Cemetery	16	Roller/Disbrow Farm Cemetery
7	Dietrich Farm Cemetery	17	Sparks Cemetery
8	Cliffside Acres Cemetery	18	West Providence Bible Baptist Church Cemetery
9	Indian Springs Cemetery	19	Williams Farm Cemetery
10	Kegg (Vaughn Williams Farm) Cemetery		

Baughman Union Church Cemetery

Documented: Summer of 2017

A special thank you to Bronwyn Graham for the information on Mary E. (Johnson) Stayer.

GPS Coordinates

39.968852, -78.346176

Address

Menchtown Road

Everett, PA 15537

Cemetery List

NUMBER	NAMES/INSCRIPTIONS	BIRTH DATE	DEATH DATE	MISC. INFO.
1	CLARA P. KARNS	MARCH 16, 1897	MARCH 7, 1981	DOUBLE STONE
2	ALBERT J. KARNS	JUNE 2, 1894	DEC. 25, 1962	
3	CHARLES A. KARNS	JULY 25, 1853	JULY 10, 1911	
4	JENNIE KARNS WIFE OF CHARLES A. KARNS	APR. 28, 1861	APR. 19, 1938	DOUBLE STONE

NUMBER	NAMES/INSCRIPTIONS	BIRTH DATE	DEATH DATE	MISC. INFO.
5	SIMON KARNS CO. K. 208 REGT. PA. VOL.	MAY 6, 1822	APR. 16, 1892	
6	MARY ANN KARNS WIFE OF SIMON KARNS AGED 59 YEARS, 4 MONTHS AND 15 DAYS		DEC. 19, 1879	
7	D. W. HOCKENBERRY	JULY 9, 1850	APR. 5, 1922	DOUBLE STONE
8	AMANDA L. HOCKENBERRY WIFE OF D. W. HOCKENBERRY	SEPT. 26, 1850	JULY 7, 1927	
9	ULYSSIS RUE HOCKENBERRY SON OF D. W. & A. L. HOCKENBERRY	FEB. 2, 1885	MAR. 4, 1887	
10	MARY C. HOCKENBERRY DAUGHTER OF D. W. & A. L. HOCKENBERRY	DEC. 22, 1873	FEB. 28, 1884	
11	MARY A. HOCKENBERRY WIFE OF J. HOCKENBERRY AGED 61 YEARS, 9 MONTHS AND 1 DAY		OCT. 6, 1882	
12	GEORGE BAUGHMAN	FEB. 28, 1804	JULY 18, 1884	DOUBLE STONE
13	MARY BAUGHMAN WIFE OF GEO. BAUGHMAN	NOV. 8, 1809	MAY 10, 1888	
14	WILLIAM J. BAUGHMAN CO. E. 2ND REG. PA CAV DIED AT WASHINGTON D.C. AGED 26 YEARS, 5 MONTHS AND 4 DAYS		APR. 26, 1864	
15	MARIA BAUGHMAN DAU. OF G. AND M. BAUGHMAN AGED 12 YEARS AND 10 DAYS		AUG. 24, 1862	
16	WILLIAM C. DIBERT SON OF J. & S. DIBERT AGED 7 YEARS, 10 MONTHS AND 13 DAYS		NOV. 17, 1871	
17	JOSIAH D. DIBERT SON OF J. & S. DIBERT AGED 5 HOURS		APR. 27, 1878	
18	SARAH DIBERT WIFE OF JOHN DIBERT AGED 53 YEARS, 8 MONTHS AND 11 DAYS		FEB. 23, 1899	

NUMBER	NAMES/INSCRIPTIONS	BIRTH DATE	DEATH DATE	MISC. INFO.
19	JOHN DIBERT AGED 64 YEARS, 3 MONTHS AND 24 DAYS		NOV. 6, 1900	
20	ALLEN RAY FEIGHT SON OF S. & A. FEIGHT	1898	1899	
21	WALTER J. DIBERT	DEC. 11, 1898	NOV. 3, 1956	
22	HARRY M. DIBERT SON OF D. W. & S. C. DIBERT AGED 5 YEARS AND 25 DAYS		SEPT. 10, 1890	
23	STELLA I. DIBERT DAU. OF D. W. & S. C. DIBERT AGED 2 YEARS, 6 MONTHS AND 19 DAYS		AUG. 17, 1896	
24	DANIEL W. DIBERT	JULY 24, 1861	AUG. 17, 1938	
25	SUSANNA C. SMITH DIBERT WIFE OF DANIEL W. DIBERT	OCT. 18, 1862	OCT. 1, 1930	DOUBLE STONE
26	DANIEL O. STAYER	DEC. 1, 1867	FEB. 25, 1939	DOUBLE STONE
27	HATTIE M. STAYER	FEB. 28, 1872	FEB. 23, 1941	
28	HATTIE STRALEY DAU. OF W. & M. STRALEY AGED 19 YEARS AND 27 DAYS		FEB. 3, 1896	
29	WILLIAM L. STRALEY AGED 56 YEARS, 9 MONTHS AND 15 DAYS			
30	CARRIE E. STAYER DAU. OF J. & S. R. STAYER AGED 8 YEARS, 6 MONTHS AND 25 DAYS		FEB. 8, 1898	
31	HOMER STAYER SON OF J. & S. R. STAYER AGED 11 MONTHS AND 20 DAYS		JAN. 20, 1898	
32	CLARA V. STAYER WIFE OF H. P. STAYER AGED 27 YEARS, 8 MONTHS AND 12 DAYS		NOV. 12, 1904	

NUMBER	NAMES/INSCRIPTIONS	BIRTH DATE	DEATH DATE	MISC. INFO.
33	OLIVE R. MCDANIEL AGED 2 YEARS AND 11 DAYS		SEPT. 1, 1888	DAUGHTERS OF G. W. & A. MCDANIEL
34	MYRTLE B. MCDANIEL AGED 18 YEARS AND 6 DAYS		SEPT. 8, 1899	
35	RENA M. MCDANIEL AGED 2 YEARS, 7 MONTHS AND 9 DAYS		JAN. 27, 1898	
36	AMANDA MCDANIEL WIFE OF G. W. MCDANIEL AGED 53 YEARS, 2 MONTHS AND 22 DAYS		SEPT. 15, 1898	
37	GEORGE W. MCDANIEL AGED 70 YEARS, 11 MONTHS AND 3 DAYS CO. C. 133RD REGT. PA VOL. BATL. S ARTL.		JAN. 25, 1915	
38	MAREA I. MCDANIEL DAU. OF G. W. & HATTIE MCDANIEL		MAY 16, 1902	
39	R. I. MCDANIEL	JUNE 18, 1906	AUG. 23, 1906	
40	R. E. MCDANIEL	JUNE 18, 1906	FEB. 11, 1907	
41	CHRISTOPHER L. STAYER	JUNE 17, 1953	NOV. 2, 1984	
42	NORA A. STAYER	OCT. 29, 1888	MAY 10, 1967	
43	JOHN S. STAYER	JULY 30, 1884	MAY 31, 1955	
44	SANFORD DRAKE	1857	1934	DOUBLE STONE
45	MARTHA OSTER DRAKE WIFE OF SANFORD DRAKE		IT IS UNKNOWN IF MARTHA IS BURIED HERE. ACCORDING TO SANFORD'S PENNSYLVANIA DEATH CERTIFICATE NUMBER 19659, HE WAS A WIDOWER. THAT MEANS THAT MARTHA WOULD HAVE DIED BEFORE FEB. 14, 1934.	
46	OLIVE E. KARNS	1885	1980	DOUBLE STONE
47	SIMON P. KARNS	1886	1964	
48	JUDITH MARIE WEICHT	1946	2010	FUNERAL HOME MARKER FROM DALLA VALLE FUNERAL HOME
49	TAMMY J. THOMAS	NOV. 21, 1973	JAN. 17, 2008	
50	CATHERINE M. WEICHT	1914	2002	DOUBLE STONE
51	FRED C. WEICHT	1911	1975	

NUMBER	NAMES/INSCRIPTIONS	BIRTH DATE	DEATH DATE	MISC. INFO.
52	LESTER W. WEICHT	1890	1975	TRIPLE STONE
53	HULDA K. WEICHT	1889	1933	
54	MARY ELLEN WEICHT INFANT DAU. OF LESTER W. AND HULDA K. WEICHT AGED 19 DAYS		1933	
55	VIRGINIA M. SWINDELL	JUNE 29, 1917	OCT. 11, 1998	
56	JOSIAH MAY	AUG. 4, 1835	MAY 12, 1875	DOUBLE STONE
57	MARY A. MAY WIFE OF JOSIAH MAY	MARCH 20, 1832	AUG. 22, 1896	
58	MARY E. (JOHNSON) STAYER AGED 34 YEARS, 11 MONTHS AND 21 DAYS	JUNE 26, 1871	JUNE 17, 1906	MARY HAS NO STONE IN THIS CEMETERY. THIS INFORMATION IS FROM PENNSYLVANIA DEATH CERTIFICATE #53282 WHICH LISTS PLACE OF BURIAL AS BAUGHMAN'S CHURCH.

NOTES

Bussard Cemetery (Warrior Ridge)

Documented: Late Summer of 2017

This cemetery is located on private property. Please ask permission from landowner prior to entering.

A special thank you to Niels Witkamp who provided information on this cemetery. Niels visited this

cemetery during the summer of 2017 and uncovered a stone for David Morris.

GPS Coordinates

39.974198, -78.398315

Address

Black Valley Road

Everett, PA 15537

Cemetery List

NUMBER	NAMES/INSCRIPTIONS	BIRTH DATE	DEATH DATE	MISC. INFO.
1	CHRISTINA BUSSARD WIFE OF JOHN BUSSARD AGED 91 YEARS, 4 MONTHS AND 21 DAYS		JULY 26, 1890	FOOTSTONE INSCRIBED C. B.
2	JACOB BUSSARD SON OF JOSEPH AND MARIA BUSSARD AGED 5 YEARS AND 5 MONTHS		AUG. 19, 1860	
3	JOHN BUSSARD AGED 79 YEARS, 8 MONTHS AND 18 DAYS		APRIL 6, 1872	FOOTSTONE INSCRIBED J. B.
4	JOSEPH E. BUSSARD AGED 85 YEARS, 7 MONTHS AND 10 DAYS		OCT. 17, 1908	FOOTSTONE INSCRIBED J. B.
5	MARIA F. MENCH BUSSARD WIFE OF JOSEPH E. BUSSARD AGED 82 YEARS, 4 MONTHS AND 12 DAYS		OCT. 12, 1905	FOOTSTONE INSCRIBED M. F. M. B.
6	SUSANNAH BUSSARD DAU. OF JOSEPH AND MARIA BUSSARD AGED 2 MONTHS AND 9 DAYS		DEC. 11, 1850	FOOTSTONE INSCRIBED S. B.
7	DAVID B. MORRIS SON OF J. S. AND S. E. MORRIS AGED 21 DAYS		NOV. 24, 1855	
8	EMMA R. WEICHT DAU. OF S. AND I. J. WRIGHT AGED 23 DAYS		OCT. 30, 1892	FOOTSTONE INSCRIBED E. R. W.
9	FIELD STONE NO INSCRIPTION			
10	SMALL STONE INSCRIBED J. M.			

NOTES

Calhoun Farm Cemetery

Documented: Summer of 2017

This cemetery is located on private property. Please ask permission from landowner prior to entering.

A special thank you to Susan Calhoun who provided me with information on this cemetery. Although I visited the cemetery, took photos and transcribed the info from my photographs, Susan also provided me with her documentation.

GPS Coordinates

39.969957, -78.358297

Address

West Mattie Road

Everett, PA 15537

Cemetery List

NUMBER	NAMES/INSCRIPTIONS	BIRTH DATE	DEATH DATE	MISC. INFO.
1	ELIZABETH CALHOUN AGED 77 YEARS, 7 MONTHS AND 15 DAYS		FEB. 12, 1922	
2	JAMES CALHOON AGED 70 YEARS, 1 MONTH AND 13 DAYS		APR. 5, 1878	
3	MARYANN C. CALHOON WIFE OF JAMES CALHOON AGED 43 YEARS, 2 MONTHS AND 10 DAYS		OCT. 30, 1857	
4	FIELD STONE NO INSCRIPTION			
5	REBECCA J. CALHOON AGED 47 YEARS, 9 MONTHS AND 17 DAYS		JAN. 16, 1900	
6	JOSEPH CALHOUN AGED 32 YEARS, 6 MONTHS AND 13 DAYS		FEB. 25, 1908	
7	CHRISTIAN CALHOUN SON OF G. H. & J. CALHOUN AGED 4 DAYS		AUG. 16, 1875	
8	GEORGE H. CALHOUN	DEC. 5, 1847	SEPT. 30, 1920	DOUBLE STONE
9	JULIAN WALLACE CALHOUN WIFE OF GEORGE H. CALHOUN	FEB. 12, 1852	OCT. 13, 1921	
10	ELLEN CALHOON AGED 75 YEARS, 7 MONTHS AND 11 DAYS		MAR. 16, 1885	
11	FIELD STONE NO INSCRIPTION			
12	REBECCA CALHOON WIFE OF J. CALHOON AGED 82 YEARS AND 8 DAYS		FEB. 2, 1867	
13	JOHN CALHOON AGED 85 YEARS, 4 MONTHS AND 14 DAYS		AUG. 15, 1864	
14	SMALL STONE NO INSCRIPTION			
15	JAMES H. CALHOUN	1871	1955	DOUBLE STONE
16	MYRTLE K. CALHOUN WIFE OF JAMES H. CALHOUN	1877	1914	
17	SMALL STONE NO INSCRIPTION			

NOTES

Cherry Lane Church Cemetery

Documented: Early 2017

GPS Coordinates

39.947732, -78.366087

Address

Cherry Lane

Clearville, PA 15535

Cemetery List

NUMBER	NAMES/INSCRIPTIONS	BIRTH DATE	DEATH DATE	MISC. INFO.
1	ALBERT KOSSA	MARCH 9, 1908	SEPT. 19, 2000	DOUBLE STONE
2	GIZELLA KOSSA	NOV. 2, 1908	OCT. 23, 1987	
3	MARGARET KOSSA	NOV. 28, 1939	JULY 6, 2002	
4	MICHAEL R. PITTMAN	JUNE 19, 1951	APRIL 7, 2017	DOUBLE STONE BROTHERS
5	RICK E. PITTMAN	NOV. 30. 1953		
6	CLAUDE E. LEVY	SEPT. 16, 1933	MAY 8, 1997	DOUBLE STONE MARRIED DEC. 10, 1954
7	GAYLE N. LEVY	JAN. 4, 1937		
8	HOWARD "BEN" WINDSOR VIETNAM	SEPT. 21, 1936	MAR. 3, 2017	
9	PAUL DALE MILLER A2C US AIR FORCE KOREA	FEB. 28, 1932	AUG. 6, 1998	
10	THADDEOUS E. PITTMAN	1908	2001	DOUBLE STONE
11	GRACE P. PITTMAN	1913	1977	
12	JOB H. MELLOTT	JULY 25, 1852	MAY 26, 1925	DOUBLE STONE
13	LYDIA BAUGHMAN MELLOTT WIFE OF JOB H. MELLOTT	FEB. 26, 1844	MARCH 23, 1926	
14	WILLARD B. GUY	MAR. 28, 1937	DEC. 23, 2008	DOUBLE STONE MARRIED AUG. 24, 1971
15	LINDA J. GUY	JULY 5, 1949		
16	MARY HARMAN	1866	1939	DOUBLE STONE
17	JOB HARMAN	1860	1930	
18	ZINA M. TRAIL	JULY 30, 1893	NOV. 17, 1946	
19	PAUL L. MEARKLE	DEC. 16, 1921	OCT. 19, 2009	DOUBLE STONE
20	G. MARIE MEARKLE	MAY 27, 1935	SEPT. 17, 1979	
21	DANIEL BENNETT	NOV. 18, 1901	APR. 26, 1975	
22	PAUL ANDREW BENNETT SON OF DANIEL AND ETHEL BENNETT	DEC. 16, 1928	DEC. 8, 1929	
23	ETHEL E. BENNETT	MAR. 26, 1898	JAN. 30, 1972	
24	JOHN A. BENNETT	DEC. 31, 1924	NOV. 6, 2004	
25	DARLENE J. PITTMAN	DEC. 31, 1946	MAR. 31, 1948	
26	MENDELL L. PITTMAN	1906	1971	DOUBLE STONE
27	PAULINE W. PITTMAN	1906	1997	
28	MYRON N. PRICE	MAY 1, 1940	OCT. 25, 2011	DOUBLE STONE MARRIED JUNE 29, 1968
30	RICHARD H. PITTMAN	JULY 9, 1935		DOUBLE STONE
31	LUCY M. PITTMAN	NOV. 5, 1941	NOV. 4, 2014	

NUMBER	NAMES/INSCRIPTIONS	BIRTH DATE	DEATH DATE	MISC. INFO.
32	ALBERT SMITH AGED 22 YEARS, 10 MONTHS AND 13 DAYS	JAN. 16, 1896	NOV. 29, 1918	
33	BESSIE SMITH COLLEDGE	NOV. 30, 1888	NOV. 1914	
34	STANLEY SMITH	1885	1968	
35	ARNOLD EUGENE CLARK SON OF CHALMER AND VESTA CLARK	NOV. 14, 1935	APR. 14, 1944	
36	CHALMER C. CLARK	JAN. 11, 1912	JUNE 14, 2005	DOUBLE STONE
37	VESTA M. CLARK	AUG. 24, 1912	AUG. 17, 1999	
38	HENRY SOLLENBERGER AGED 77 YEARS		MAR. 23, 1924	DOUBLE STONE
39	LEANNA SNOWBERGER SOLLENBERGER AGED 64 YEARS AND 20 DAYS		FEB. 7, 1918	
40	INFANT KOONTZ SON OF D. G. & N. S. KOONTZ		MAY 15, 1922	
41	VIRGINIA M. MCLAUGHLIN	1918	2000	DOUBLE STONE
42	HELEN L. BASS	1931		SISTERS
43	J. HOWARD PITTMAN	JULY 20, 1879	JAN. 25, 1957	DOUBLE STONE
44	MARY D. PITTMAN	MAR. 4, 1890	FEB. 7, 1966	
45	NORA E. PITTMAN	NOV. 3, 1913	FEB. 9, 1944	
46	HIMES GRUBB	JAN. 20, 1845	JAN. 12, 1897	DOUBLE STONE
47	FANNIE SNOWBERGER GRUBB WIFE OF HIMES GRUBB	NOV. 30, 1849	JULY 25, 1920	
48	STELLA S. GRUBB DAU. OF H. & F. GRUBB AGED 1 YEAR, 5 MONTHS AND 13 DAYS		FEB. 16, 1895	
49	MARY JANE GRUBB DAU. OF HIMES & FANNIE GRUBB AGED 22 YEARS, 9 MONTHS AND 5 DAYS		OCT. 2, 1895	
50	RUTH PITTMAN	SEPT. 24, 1929	SEPT. 28, 1947	
51	NAOMI WELKER DAVIS WIFE	NOV. 16, 1917	JAN. 29, 1996	TRIPLE STONE
52	ANDREW LEO DAVIS HUSBAND	SEPT. 30, 1913	OCT. 19, 1981	
53	DORIS ANN DAVIS DAUGHTER	MARCH 14, 1939	DEC. 18, 1953	

NUMBER	NAMES/INSCRIPTIONS	BIRTH DATE	DEATH DATE	MISC. INFO.
54	ANDREW SNOWBERGER AGED 61 YEARS AND 1 DAY	JULY 6, 1842	JULY 7, 1903	DOUBLE STONE
55	CATHARINE RITCHEY SNOWBERGER AGED 83 YEARS, 11 MONTHS AND 18 DAYS	MAY 5, 1849	APR. 23, 1933	
56	LILLIAN B. DAVIS	JULY 19, 1893	MAY 17, 1977	DOUBLE STONE
57	HARRY C. DAVIS	OCT. 19, 1888	DEC. 6, 1970	
58	FRANKLIN ROY DIBERT	AUG. 12, 1887	SEPT. 15, 1958	
59	INFANT DIBERT DAU. OF ROY AND REDA DIBERT AGED 6 DAYS		JUNE 13, 1911	
60	CORA REDA DIBERT	JAN. 4, 1891	MAY 21, 1970	
61	EARL M. RITCHEY	1909	1981	DOUBLE STONE
62	ISA B. RITCHEY	1913	1999	
63	JOHN B. SMITH	1821	1910	DOUBLE STONE
64	NANCY CLAPPER SMITH WIFE OF JOHN B. SMITH	1823	1910	
65	GEORGE R. PRICE PVT US ARMY WORLD WAR I	JAN. 14, 1895	NOV. 21, 1984	DOUBLE STONE
66	FANNIE A. PRICE	OCT. 6, 1898	DEC. 20, 1936	
67	SAMUEL SOLLENBERGER	AUG. 26, 1819	NOV. 1, 1902	DOUBLE STONE
68	CATHARINE SNYDER SOLLENBERGER WIFE OF SAMUEL SOLLENBERGER	NOV. 28, 18	OCT. 15, 1906	
69	JANET C. PRICE	1926	1927	TRIPLE STONE CHILDREN OF G. R. & F. A. PRICE
70	LEE A. PRICE	1927	1929	
71	JOE PRICE		1938	
72	ANDREW GARLICK	1868	1942	DOUBLE STONE
73	ELMIRA GARLICK WIFE OF ANDREW GARLICK	1861	1922	
74	ALLEN B. RITCHEY	MAR. 21, 1904	JULY 19, 1924	TRIPLE STONE
75	ANNIE J. RITCHEY	MAY 15, 1867	JAN. 23, 1927	
76	ANDREW RITCHEY	JUNE 11, 1870	MAY 1, 1937	
77	WILLA MAE RITCHEY DAU. OF A. & A. J. RITCHEY		NOV. 27, 1907	
78	HANNAH E. BOWEN BEELER WIFE OF SAMUEL V. BEELER	DEC. 30. 1860	DEC. 4, 1944	
79	CHARLES L. BEELER	JAN. 20, 1881	OCT. 26, 1949	

NUMBER	NAMES/INSCRIPTIONS	BIRTH DATE	DEATH DATE	MISC. INFO.
80	HARRY M. RITCHEY WORLD WAR I	1896	1965	
81	FRANK M. RITCHEY	1899	1968	
82	OTIS E. JAY	1909	1983	DOUBLE
83	MARY V. JAY	1907	1997	STONE
84	SHARON NADINE JAY DAU. OF PAUL & NANCY JAY	SEPT. 25, 1958	MAY 15, 1963	
85	WILLIAM EMERSON PITTMAN INFANT SON OF GEORGE W. & JANE PITTMAN	MARCH 2, 1927	MARCH 20, 1927	
86	ULYSSES G. PITTMAN	NOV. 12, 1864	FEB. 20, 1941	DOUBLE
87	ELIZA P. PITTMAN	OCT. 2, 1877	NOV. 11, 1900	STONE
88	FRANCIS E. PITTMAN	OCT. 6, 1872	NOV. 4, 1928	
89	JENNIE D. PITTMAN	MAR. 30, 1874	MAY 24, 1933	QUADRUPLE STONE
90	JOHN C. PITTMAN	JUNE 30, 1908	DEC. 22, 1983	
91	ROY PITTMAN INFANT		MAY 21, 1906	
92	LEVI C. SMITH	NOV. 15, 1853	MAR. 12, 1933	
93	ALLIE J. SMITH WIFE OF LEVI C. SMITH		NOV. 30, 1894	
94	LILLY SMITH DAU. OF L. C. & M. E. SMITH AGED 8 MONTHS AND 3 DAYS		DEC. 1, 1901	
95	SARA SMITH DAU. OF L. C. & M. E. SMITH		JAN. 13, 1915	
96	HERBERT R. SMITH SON OF L. C. & A. J. SMITH	JAN. 25, 1884	SEPT. 10, 1919	
97	MARY E. WHITFIELD SMITH WIFE OF LEVI C. SMITH AGED 47 YEARS AND 29 DAYS		APR. 12, 1923	
98	WILLIAM H. WHITE III	SEPT. 18, 1961		DOUBLE
99	CHRISTINA JO WHITE	OCT. 17, 1965	MAY 9, 2015	STONE
100	TIMOTHY SHANE CRAIG		JULY 21, 1995	
101	JOHN H. STANTON	SEPT. 24, 1931	MAY 25, 1996	DOUBLE
102	BETTY G. STANTON	MAY 17, 1932		STONE
103	KENNETH D. MELLOTT	FEB. 19, 1916	JUNE 15, 1996	DOUBLE
104	MARIE V. MELLOTT	SEPT. 13, 1915	DEC. 27, 2001	STONE
105	MERRIT M. BOWMAN	APR. 3, 1940		DOUBLE
106	M. ALICE BOWMAN	JULY 13, 1943	JUNE 21, 2000	STONE
107	CINDY M. COGAN	OCT. 21, 1951	MAY 4, 1984	

NUMBER	NAMES/INSCRIPTIONS	BIRTH DATE	DEATH DATE	MISC. INFO.
108	KENNETH A. BOWMAN	MAR. 15, 1917	OCT. 26, 1999	DOUBLE STONE
109	VERNA G. SOLLENBERGER BOWMAN	DEC. 14, 1919	OCT. 16, 1999	
110	GLENN D. KLAHRE	DEC. 8, 1920	AUG. 10, 2006	DOUBLE STONE
111	DONNA W. KLAHRE	MAY 1, 1934		
112	DAVID L. KLAHRE	OCT. 8, 1957	AUG. 23, 1987	
113	ROBERT L. DIBERT	DEC. 27, 1919	MAY 22, 1994	DOUBLE STONE
114	BETTY A. DIBERT	FEB. 16, 1919	DEC. 13, 1994	
115	MARVIN CALHOUN WORLD WAR II	OCT. 3, 1924	APRIL 2, 2017	
116	W. HOWARD FLEEGLE	JAN. 28, 1912	JULY 31, 1997	DOUBLE STONE
117	MILDRED B. FLEEGLE	OCT. 18, 1914	NOV. 27, 1996	
118	ROBERT GOGOLLA	JUNE 18, 1907	SEPT. 8, 1986	DOUBLE STONE
119	CATHERINE E. GOGOLLA	MAR. 15, 1913	SEPT. 18, 1982	
120	WILLIAM L. GROVER, SR. CPL US ARMY AIR CORPS WORLD WAR II	SEPT. 18, 1920	AUG. 6, 1987	
121	MARILYN B. GROVER	DEC. 4, 1928	MARCH 9, 2017	
122	LEO V. PITTMAN PVT US ARMY WORLD WAR II	MAR. 26, 1925	JULY 2, 2007	DOUBLE STONE
123	M. MARTHA PITTMAN	JULY 11, 1929	NOV. 17, 2011	
124	DANIEL L. PITTMAN	JAN. 16, 1954		
125	RAYMOND E. "BUTCH" CRAIG	JAN. 22, 1940	MAY 10, 2011	DOUBLE STONE
126	LORETTA E. CRAIG	SEPT. 27, 1940	FEB. 23, 2010	

NOTES

Clark Farm Cemetery

Documented: Early 2018

This cemetery is located on private property. Please ask permission from landowner prior to entering.

Thank you to Susan Calhoun for helping me to locate this cemetery.

This cemetery once had a fence surrounding it with a gate, pieces of it are still visible. The cemetery needs a lot of work or there will be no trace of it in a few years. There is a large space between graves indicating many unmarked graves.

GPS Coordinates

39.945166, -78.328348

Address

1681 West Mattie Road

Everett, PA 15537

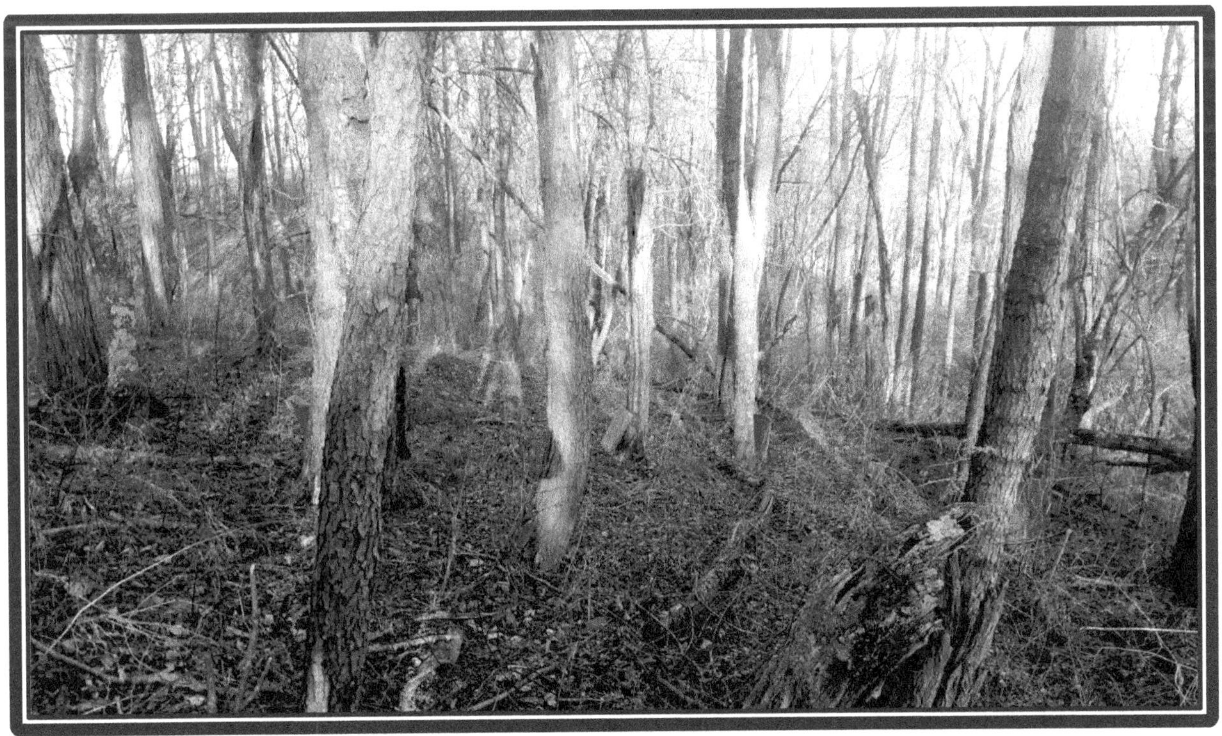

Cemetery List

NUMBER	NAMES/INSCRIPTIONS	BIRTH DATE	DEATH DATE	MISC. INFO.
1	DAVID CLARK AGED 60 YEARS, 8 MONTHS AND 12 DAYS		OCT. 15, 1859	STONE STILL STANDING. FOOTSTONE INSCRIBED D. C.
2	JOEL CLARK AGED 63 YEARS, 6 MONTHS AND 20 DAYS		OCT. 5, 1864	STONE STILL STANDING FOOTSTONE INSCRIBED J C.
3	REBECCA CLARK WIFE OF JOEL CLARK AGED 25 YEARS AND 1 MONTH		JULY 7, 1834	THIS STONE WAS LAYING FLAT ON THE GROUND AND MOSTLY BURIED. IF YOU ARE STANDING IN FRONT OF JOEL'S STONE, REBECCA'S STONE IS LOCATED TO THE RIGHT.
4	REBECCA CLARK DAU. OF J. AND M. CLARK AGED 18 YEARS, 2 MONTHS AND 2 DAYS		SEPT. 24, 1864	STONE STILL STANDING FOOTSTONE INSCRIBED R. C.
5	RHODA HANN WIFE OF H. HANN AGED 38 YEARS, _____ MONTHS AND ______ DAYS		MAY 1__, 18__	THIS STONE IS BROKEN IN HALF AND WORN. MOSTLY UNREADABLE. IT WAS STANDING UP NEXT TO A TREE.
6	FIELD STONE NO INSCRIPTION			
7	FIELD STONE NO INSCRIPTION			
8	FIELD STONE NO INSCRIPTION			
9	FIELD STONE NO INSCRIPTION			
10	FIELD STONE NO INSCRIPTION			

Cliffside Acres Cemetery

Documented: Early 2018

This cemetery is located on private property. Please ask permission from landowner prior to entering.

GPS Coordinates

40.035226, -78.309367

Address

West Graceville Road

Everett, PA 15537

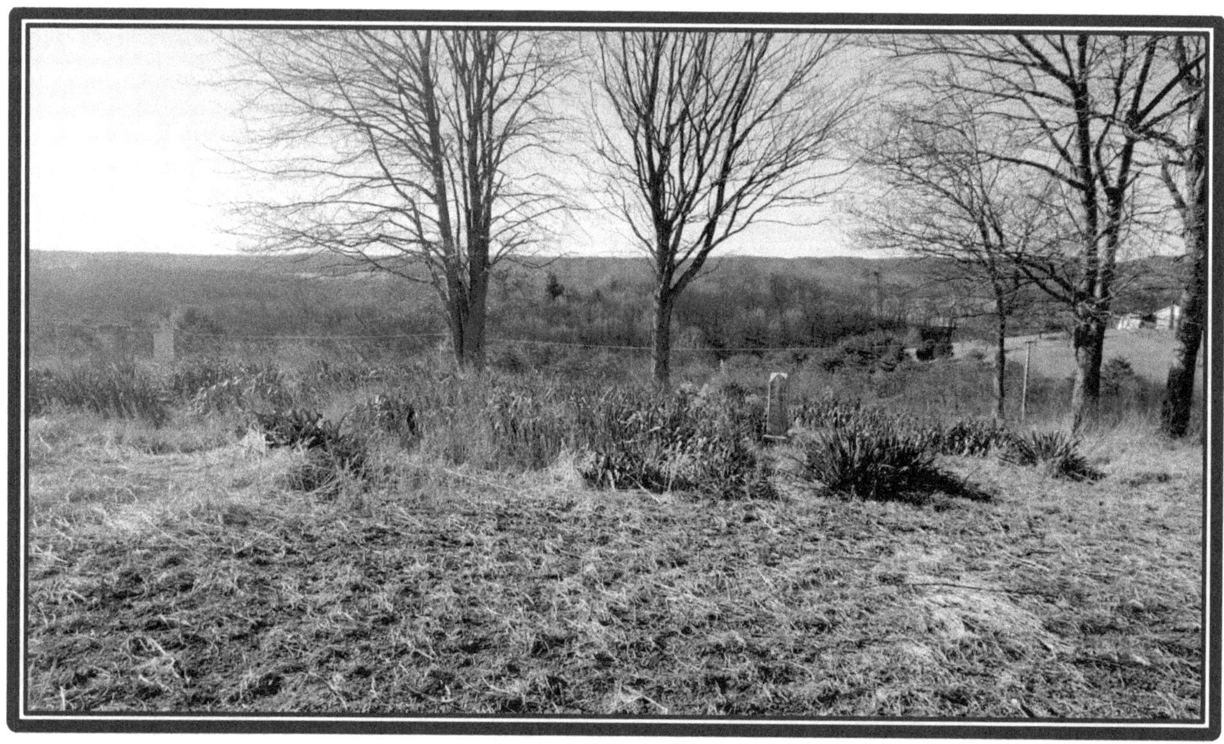

Cemetery List

NUMBER	NAMES/INSCRIPTIONS	BIRTH DATE	DEATH DATE	MISC. INFO.
1	ELIZABETH LEADER COOK WIFE OF EZEKIEL COOK AGED 84 YEARS AND 2 DAYS		APRIL 13, 1874	
2	EZEKIEL COOK, SR. AGED 85 YEARS, 9 MONTHS AND 23 DAYS	APRIL 8, 1783	FEB. 1, 1869	
3	WILLIAM LINCOLN COOK SON OF EZEKIEL AND MATILDA COOK AGED 2 YEARS, 3 MONTHS AND 1 DAY		JULY 1, 1863	
4	JACOB C. FOOR AGED 75 YEARS, 5 MONTHS AND 21 DAYS		AUG. 13, 1884	DOUBLE STONE
5	CATHARINE FOOR WIFE OF J. C. FOOR AGED 84 YEARS AND 5 MONTHS		OCT. 11, 1882	
6	THOMAS CULVER SON OF J. H. AND M. CULVER AGED 3 YEARS, 4 MONTHS AND 12 DAYS		JAN. __, 1870	
7	HOWARD B. FOOR SON OF J. R. AND T. FOOR AGED 4 YEARS AND 25 DAYS		NOV. 11, 1880	
8	JAMES HARMAN MANSPEARKER SON OF JACOB AND SUSAN MANSPEAKER AGED 1 YEAR, 11 MONTHS AND 27 DAYS		MAY 22, 1855	

NOTES

Dibert Farm Cemetery

Documented: Early 2017

This cemetery is located on private property. Please ask permission from landowner prior to entering.

GPS Coordinates

39.980256, -78.334748

Address

Sollenberger Road

Everett, PA 15537

Cemetery List

NUMBER	NAMES/INSCRIPTIONS	BIRTH DATE	DEATH DATE	MISC. INFO.
1	PETER KARN AGED 87 YEARS AND 7 DAYS		NOV. 12, 1866	FOOTSTONE
2	SARAH KARN WIFE OF PETER KARN AGED 66 YEARS, 7 MONTHS AND 20 DAYS		DEC. 30, 1853	FOOTSTONE

Dietrich Farm Cemetery

Documented: Fall of 2017

This cemetery is located on private property. Please ask permission from landowner prior to entering.

GPS Coordinates

39.961689, -78.338007

Address

Hidden Hollow Lane

Everett, PA 15537

Cemetery List

NUMBER	NAMES/INSCRIPTIONS	BIRTH DATE	DEATH DATE	MISC. INFO.
1	BOBBY LINDEN HUGGINS US NAVY VIETNAM	AUG. 16, 1941	MAY 24, 1997	DOUBLE STONE 
2	CAROL LYNN HUGGINS		LIVING	
3	JEROME M. DIETRICH CM3 US NAVY WORLD WAR II	AUG. 20, 1925	FEB. 26, 1986	DOUBLE STONE
4	JANE B. DIETRICH	OCT. 23, 1923	FEB. 15, 1998	
5	ROSS WILLIAM BRANTNER II	JAN. 29, 1977	OCT. 3, 2004	
6	JUDY E. (DIETRICH) DILLOW	JUNE 13, 1949	OCT. 30, 2009	DOUBLE STONE
7	JOE D. DILLOW		LIVING	

NOTES

Indian Springs Cemetery

Documented: Summer of 2017

This cemetery is located on private property. Please ask permission from landowner prior to entering.

Thank you to the Bedford County Historical Society for providing me with a map and survey of the

cemetery to reference after my documentation of this cemetery. I used the information that was on the

map to compare to what I had already documented from the cemetery. Please reference the cemetery

listing on the following pages for notes on graves that I did not find in the cemetery but were listed on

the map and survey.

GPS Coordinates

    39.961795, -78.412510

Address

    Black Valley Road

    Everett, PA 15537

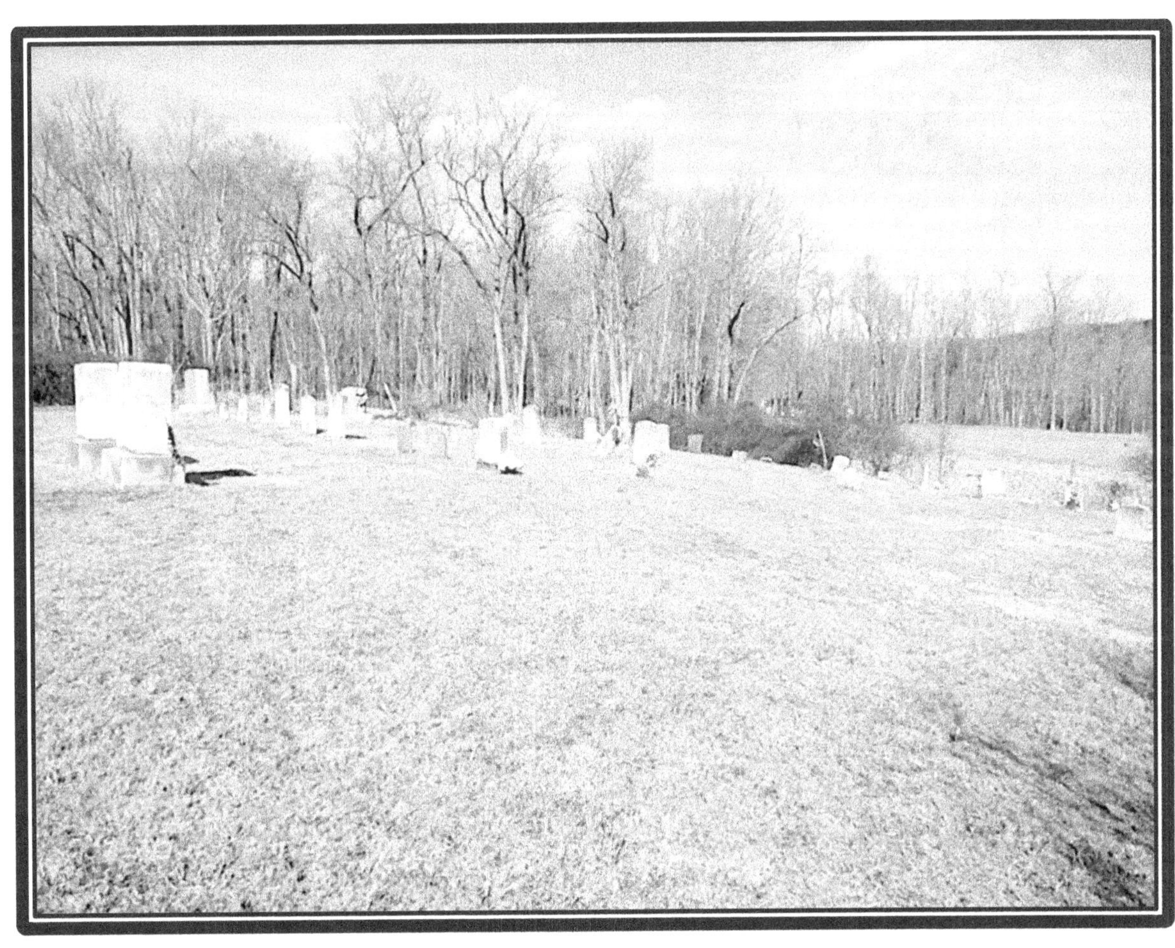

Cemetery List

NUMBER	NAMES/INSCRIPTIONS	BIRTH DATE	DEATH DATE	MISC. INFO.
1	FIELD STONE NO INSCRIPTION			
2	FIELD STONE NO INSCRIPTION			
3	HAROLD R. BISHOP SON OF H. & J. A. BISHOP AGED 3 MONTHS		MAR. 1, 1902	
4	ROY BISHOP SON OF CLYDE AND ANNA BISHOP	JUNE 8, 1907	SEPT. 8, 1908	STONE IS FLAT ON THE GROUND AND PARTIALLY COVERED. INFO IS FROM PA DEATH CERTIFICATE # 85817
5	FIELD STONE NO INSCRIPTION			
6	WILLIAM H. SMITH AGED 69 YEARS, 11 MONTHS AND 4 DAYS CO. K 208TH REGT. PA VOL.		FEB. 4, 1915	
7	MARY J. SMITH WIFE OF WILLIAM H. SMITH AGED 73 YEARS AND 3 DAYS		FEB. 13, 1910	
8	BENJAMIN F. SMITH SON OF WILLIAM H. AND M. J. SMITH AGED 17 YEARS, 9 MONTHS AND 11 DAYS		FEB. 16, 1896	
9	FRED SMITH			STONE WITH BLACK LETTERING
10	VALENTINE STECKMAN CO. B 2ND PA RIF. WAR OF 1812			
11	STONE WITH BLACK LETTERING			
12	HILLERY SMITH	1816	1897	
13	LEANNA RACHEL SMITH	1818	1896	DOUBLE STONE DAUGHTER OF JOHN A. & REBECCA SMITH DATES ARE APPROXIMATE

NUMBER	NAMES/INSCRIPTIONS	BIRTH DATE	DEATH DATE	MISC. INFO.
14	STONE WITH BLACK LETTERING			
15	FIELD STONE NO INSCRIPTION			
16	JOHN B. SUMMERVILLE CIVIL WAR	AUG. 31, 1828	JUNE 21, 1887	
17	JOHN SOMERVILL SON OF JOHN E. & SARAH SOMERVILL AGED 7 YEARS AND 11 MONTHS	JAN 28, 1864		DOUBLE STONE
18	ANNA JANE SOMERVILL AGED 5 MONTHS			
19	HENRIETTA SOMERVILL DAU. OF JOHN & SARAH SOMERVILL AGE 5 YEARS	JULY 24, 1868		
20	JOSEPH SPARKS AGED 73 YEARS	MAR. 25, 1754	SEPT. 18, 1827	THIS IS A CARVED FIELD STONE WAR OF 1812
21	BARBARA SPARKS AGED 16 YEARS AND 9 MONTHS		MAY 30, 1838	
22	JOSEPH SPARKS U.S. SOLDIER REV WAR			
23	ELIZABETH SPARKS AGED APPROX. 59 YEARS		MAR. 16, 1803	
24	JOHN STECKMAN AGED 88 YEARS		SEPT. 9, 1838	
25	STONE WITH BLACK LETTERING			
26	JNO. STECKMAN CO B 2ND PA RIF. WAR OF 1812			
27	ANDREW STECKMAN	MAR. 14, 1795	DEC. 13, 1827	THIS IS A CARVED STONE
28	ANNA R. DAVIS DAU. OF WILLIAM W. AND S. J. DAVIS AGED 3 YEARS, 2 MONTHS AND 4 DAYS		AUG. 16, 1886	

NUMBER	NAMES/INSCRIPTIONS	BIRTH DATE	DEATH DATE	MISC. INFO.
29	NELLIE GRACE SPARKS DAU. OF S. J. & DORA H. SPARKS AGED 2 YEARS, 4 MONTHS AND 23 DAYS		NOV. 21, 1910	
30	AARON STAYER	1810	1885	DOUBLE STONE
31	MARY ANN DEFIBAUGH STAYER	1818	1901	
32	FIELD STONE NO INSCRIPTION			
33	ELIJAH MORRIS CO. B 2ND PA RIF. WAR OF 1812			
34	ELIZABETH SPARKS AGED 71 YEARS, 1 MONTH AND 4 DAYS		JULY 28, 1858	
35	JOSEPH SPARKS, SR. CO. B 2ND PA RIF. WAR OF 1812			
36	CHRISTINA SPARKS AGED 89 YEARS AND 11 DAYS		OCT. 1, 1871	
37	SMALL FIELD STONE NO INSCRIPTION			
38	SMALL FIELD STONE NO INSCRIPTION			
39	FIELD STONE NO INSCRIPTION			
40	ABRAHAM W. SPARKS AGED 60 YEARS, 10 MONTHS AND 2 DAYS		APR. 11, 1916	
41	FIELD STONE NO INSCRIPTION			
42	FIELD STONE NO INSCRIPTION			
43	SMALL STONE NO INSCRIPTION			
44	REBECCA SPARKS AGED 89 YEARS, 2 MONTHS AND 29 DAYS	MAY 16, 1816	AUG. 15, 1905	
45	SARAH E. SPARKS DAU. OF J. AND R. SPARKS AGED 35 YEARS, 4 MONTHS AND 10 DAYS		FEB. 4, 1878	
46	JOHN SPARKS AGED 77 YEARS, 4 MONTHS AND 26 DAYS WAR OF 1812		AUG. 30. 1876	

NUMBER	NAMES/INSCRIPTIONS	BIRTH DATE	DEATH DATE	MISC. INFO.
47	MATHEW P. SPARKS SON OF J. & R. SPARKS AGED 11 YEARS, 11 MONTHS AND 18 DAYS		MAR. 24, 1858	
48	JAMES SPARKS SON OF J. & R. SPARKS AGED 4 YEARS, 9 MONTHS AND 16 DAYS		MAR. 15, 1858	
49	PHINEAS SPARKS SON OF J. AND R. SPARKS AGED 18 DAYS		MAR. 10, 1856	
50	HENRY I. RINARD, JR.	AUG. 16, 1927	FEB. 26, 1995	DOUBLE STONE
51	MARION S. RINARD	DEC. 17, 1927	AUG. 17, 2015	
52	AARON D. STAYER	MAY 4, 1854	JULY 10, 1933	DOUBLE STONE
53	MARY C. SPARKS STAYER	MAY 24, 1857	SEPT. 10, 1927	
54	GEORGE SMOUSE	1866	1938	
55	SAMUEL B. SPARKS	1848	1914	DOUBLE STONE
56	MARY M. SPARKS	1856	1932	
57	CHARLES C. SPARKS SGT. CO. L 18 BN I. R. – T. C. PVT TROOP B PA STATE CONSTABULARY WORLD WAR I	1892	1921	
58	SMALL STONE WITH BLACK LETTERING			

THE FOLLOWING GRAVES WERE LISTED ON A SURVERY MAP OF THE CEMETERY DONE BY W. HAYES CUNARD, EVERETT, PENNSYLVANIA, DATED JUNE 26, 1957. THE MAP WAS PROVIDED TO ME AT THE BEDFORD COUNTY HISTORICAL SOCIETY. ACCORDING TO THE MAP THE FOLLOWING PEOPLE ARE BURIED IN UNMARKED GRAVES IN THE CEMETERY. NO DATES WERE AVAILABLE.

NUMBER	NAMES/INSCRIPTIONS	BIRTH DATE	DEATH DATE	MISC. INFO.
59	ZELMA WEICHT			
60	AARON SPARKS			
61	WILLIAM SPARKS			
62	DAVID SPARKS			
63	RUBEN SPARKS			
64	ROBERT WEICHT			
65	ROY WEICHT			
66	VELMA WEICHT			
67	RICHARD WEICHT			
68	BERTHA WEICHT			
69	MRS. MORRIS			
70	PHILIP MORRIS			
71	MRS. ELIJAH MORRIS			
72	MRS. JOHN STECKMAN			
73	MARY SMITH			THIS IS IN ADDITION TO MARY SMITH, WIFE OF WILLIAM H. SMITH.
74	INFANT JOHNSON			
75	INFANT JOHNSON			

NOTES

NOTES

Kegg Cemetery (Vaughn Williams Farm Cemetery)

Documented: Summer of 2017

This cemetery is located on private property. Please ask permission from landowner prior to entering.

GPS Coordinates

39.981961, -78.318288

Address

Anderson Road

Everett, PA 15537

Cemetery List

NUMBER	NAMES/INSCRIPTIONS	BIRTH DATE	DEATH DATE	MISC. INFO.
1	SEBASTIAN KEGG	1811	1876	THIS STONE HAS SEVEN (7) PEOPLE LISTED ON IT. FOUR (4) ON ONE SIDE AND THREE (3) ON THE REVERSE.
2	AHIMAAZ KEGG	1853	1854	
3	AMANDA KEGG	1849	1857	
4	JOB KEGG	1843	1858	
5	ANDREW KEGG	1838	1859	
6	ENOS KEGG	1851	1858	
7	SIMON KEGG	1836	1859	
8	EVE WEAVERLING WIFE OF J. WEAVERLING AGED 62 YEARS, 1 MONTHS AND 23 DAYS		MAR. 16, 1845	
9	JACOB WEAVERLING AGED 80 YEARS, 3 MONTHS AND 16 DAYS		MAY 10, 1863	
10	JOSEPH WEAVERLING AGED 82 YEARS, 11 MONTHS AND 1 DAYS		AUG. 19, 1907	DOUBLE STONE
11	ELIZABETH MELLIN WEAVERLING WIFE OF JOSEPH WEAVERLING AGED 38 YEARS, 5 MONTHS AND 1 DAY		AUG. 11, 1868	
12	ANNA E. BARNDOLLAR DAU. OF W. H. BARNDOLLAR AGED 23 YEARS, 2 MONTHS AND 5 DAYS		DEC. 17, 1872	
13	MARY ELIZABETH IRONS DAU. OF J. IRONS AGED 4 MONTHS		SEPT. 8, 1859	
14	MAGGIE PERRIN WIFE OF NERI PERRIN AGED 38 YEARS AND 21 DAYS		SEPT. 1, 1895	
15	EVE PRICE WIFE OF J. PRICE LATER WIFE OF J. WEAVERLING	1823	1918	
16	JOHN PRICE AGED 36 YEARS CO. A 184TH REGT CIVIL WAR		MAR. 22, 1865	
17	ABRAHAM L. PRICE SON OF J. & E. PRICE AGED 8 MONTHS AND 11 DAYS		SEPT. 10, 1861	

NUMBER	NAMES/INSCRIPTIONS	BIRTH DATE	DEATH DATE	MISC. INFO.
18	ELIZABETH WEAVERLING WIFE OF PETER WEAVERLING AGED 23 YEARS, 4 MONTHS AND 8 DAYS		SEPT. 15, 1813	
19	PETER WEAVERLING AGED 68 YEARS, 3 MONTHS AND 18 DAYS		JULY 25, 1854	
20	ANN MARY WEAVERLING WIFE OF PETER WEAVERLING AGED 78 YEARS, 5 MONTHS AND 2 DAYS		OCT. 29, 1872	
21	REBECCA WEAVERLING DAU. OF PETER AND ANN MARY WEAVERLING AGED 11 YEARS, 11 MONTHS AND 19 DAYS		SEPT. 21, 1828	THIS STONE IS IN VERY POOR CONDITION AND IS CHIPPING AWAY.
22	MARY WEAVERLING DAU. OF PETER AND ANN MARY WEAVERLING AGED 10 YEARS, 11 MONTHS AND 7 DAYS		SEPT. 15, 1826	

NOTES

McDaniel Family Cemetery

Documented: Fall of 2017

This cemetery is located on private property. Please ask permission from landowner prior to entering.

Currently the land is owned by Lampire Biological Laboratories.

I visited this cemetery during the fall of 2017 and found only field stones in this cemetery. It is very

overgrown and has groundhog holes located throughout.

Thank you to Niels Witkamp who visited this cemetery several years prior and provided me with

information. Information in this cemetery listing is also from a reading of the cemetery done in the early

1900's that was made available to me, the listing did not state who documented the cemetery.

GPS Coordinates

     39.949360, -78.380019

Address

     Clear Ridge Road

     Everett, PA 15537

Cemetery List

NUMBER	NAMES/INSCRIPTIONS	BIRTH DATE	DEATH DATE	MISC. INFO.
1	AMOS MCDANIEL		SEPT. 14, 1838	
2	ANNA MCDANIEL		JULY 11, 1827	
3	ELIZABETH MCDANIEL WIFE OF JAMES MCDANIEL AGED 46 YEARS, 2 MONTHS AND 21 DAYS		JAN. 4, 1853	THIS STONE WAS IN THE CEMETERY IN 2012.
4	JAMES MCDANIEL	1805	JULY 30, 1860	
5	JOHN MCDANIEL SON OF JAMES AND ELIZABETH MCDANIEL AGED 15 YEARS, 1 MONTH AND 2 DAYS		APRIL 27, 1863	THIS STONE WAS IN THE CEMETERY IN 2012.
6	RUBEN MCDANIEL		JULY 31, 1894	
7	WILLIAM MCDANIEL		JUNE 8, 1781	
8	GEORGE W. O'NEAL SON OF AMELIA A. O'NEAL AGED 6 MONTHS AND 9 DAYS		OCT. 29, 1857	THIS STONE WAS IN THE CEMETERY IN 2012.
9	LAURA B. O'NEAL		MAY 12, 1862	

NOTES

NOTES

Morgart and Morgret Cemetery

Documented: Fall of 2017

This cemetery is located on private property. Please ask permission from landowner prior to entering.

GPS Coordinates

40.020159, -78.320418

Address

Woy Bridge Road

Everett, PA 15537

Cemetery List

NUMBER	NAMES/INSCRIPTIONS	BIRTH DATE	DEATH DATE	MISC. INFO.
1	IRENE MORGART KOONTZ AGED 23 YEARS, 7 MONTHS AND 13 DAYS		APRIL 26, 1900	
2	FRANKLIN MORGART AGED 3 YEARS, 2 MONTHS AND 22 DAYS		AUG. 16, 1870	
3	ANDREW J. MORGART AGED 46 YEARS, 6 MONTHS AND 10 DAYS		AUG. 19, 1870	
4	REBECCA O'NEAL MORGART WIFE OF A. J. MORGART AGED 74 YEARS, 1 MONTH AND 25 DAYS		APRIL 29, 1898	
5	REBECCA J. MORGART DAU. OF A. J. AND R. MORGART AGED 22 YEARS, 4 MONTHS AND 1 DAY		MAY 20, 1876	

NUMBER	NAMES/INSCRIPTIONS	BIRTH DATE	DEATH DATE	MISC. INFO.
6	PHILIP M. WHETSTONE AGED 12 YEARS 6 MONTHS AND 24 DAYS		JAN. 12, 1869	DOUBLE STONE
7	JOSEPH C. WHETSTONE AGED 5 DAYS		JULY 13, 1865	
8	MARY N. BOWMAN DAU. OF R. AND C. S. BOWMAN AGED 2 YEARS AND 2 DAYS		JULY 30, 1901	
9	MARY MORGART WIFE OF B. MORGART AGED 76 YEARS, 3 MONTHS AND 26 DAYS		JULY 6, 1874	
10	BALTZER MORGART AGED 68 YEARS, 7 MONTHS AND 20 DAYS	APRIL 29, 1785	DEC. 19, 1853	
11	ANN ELIZA MOGART DAU. OF BALTZER AND MARY MORGART AGED 13 YEARS, 11 MONTHS AND 21 DAYS	JULY 19, 1834	JUNE 10, 1848	
12	PETER MORGART, SR. AGED 88 YEARS, 6 MONTHS AND 28 DAYS	APRIL 18, 1758	NOV. 16, 1846	REV. WAR
13	CHRISTIANA MORGART	MARCH 1761	FEB. 6, 1839	
14	CATHERINE BARTON WIFE OF GEORGE BARTON AGED 76 YEARS, 5 MONTHS AND 13 DAYS		AUG. 23, 1863	
15	ALICE B. MANSPEAKER MORGART WIFE OF JEFF MORGART	1859	1894	
16	WILLIAM H. JEFF MORGART	MAY 11, 1853	SEPT. 12, 1932	
17	MARGARET MORGRET WIFE OF WILLIAM H. MORGRET AGED 51 YEARS AND 29 DAYS	FEB. 25, 1817	MAR 24, 1868	
18	MARGARET MORGART WIFE OF ABRAM MORGART AGED 51 YEARS, 2 MONTHS AND 4 DAYS		MAR. 6, 1880	
19	ABRAM MORGART AGED 42 YEARS AND 2 MONTHS	NOV. 20, 1819	JAN. 20, 1865	

NUMBER	NAMES/INSCRIPTIONS	BIRTH DATE	DEATH DATE	MISC. INFO.
20	CARL P. MORGART AGED 3 SON OF A. J. AND AMANDA HECKMAN MORGART			
21	PETER O. MORGRET AGED 30 YEARS, 6 MONTHS AND 24 DAYS	APRIL 6, 1811	OCT. 30, 1841	
22	PHILIP MORGART SON OF PETER AND CHRISTIANA MORGART	SEPT. 2, 1780	JAN. 25, 1840	
23	GEORGE BARTON AGED 45 YEARS AND 8 MONTHS		DEC. 13, 1825	
24	HENRY DEAL AGED 71 YEARS AND 9 MONTHS	APRIL 21, 1787	JAN. 21, 1859	
25	M 1890 MARIDILEN EINETOGER VONHE			
26	MARY MORGART DAU. OF BALZER AND MARY MORGART	NOV. 23, 1825	SEPT. 25, 1829	
27	DAVID BUCK AGED 66 YEARS, 4 MONTHS AND 29 DAYS		MAR. 4, 1865	
28	JACOB I. FOOR CO. K 208TH REGT. P. V. I. AGED 68 YEARS, 5 MONTHS AND 16 DAYS CIVIL WAR		FEB. 8, 1888	
29	MARY BUCK	OCT. 12, 1800	JULY 12, 1879	
30	REBECCA CONNER WIFE OF J. CONNER			STONE IS LAYING FLAT AND ONLY THE TOP HALF OF THE STONE IS LEFT

NOTES

Mount Union Christian Church Cemetery

Thank you to Susan Calhoun for providing the information on this cemetery. Although I visited, took photographs, and walked through the cemetery a few times with Susan, she provided this information to me after her documentation was complete. This listing is complete as of February 2018.

GPS Coordinates

39.973562, -78.322793

Address

Menchtown Road

Everett, PA 15537

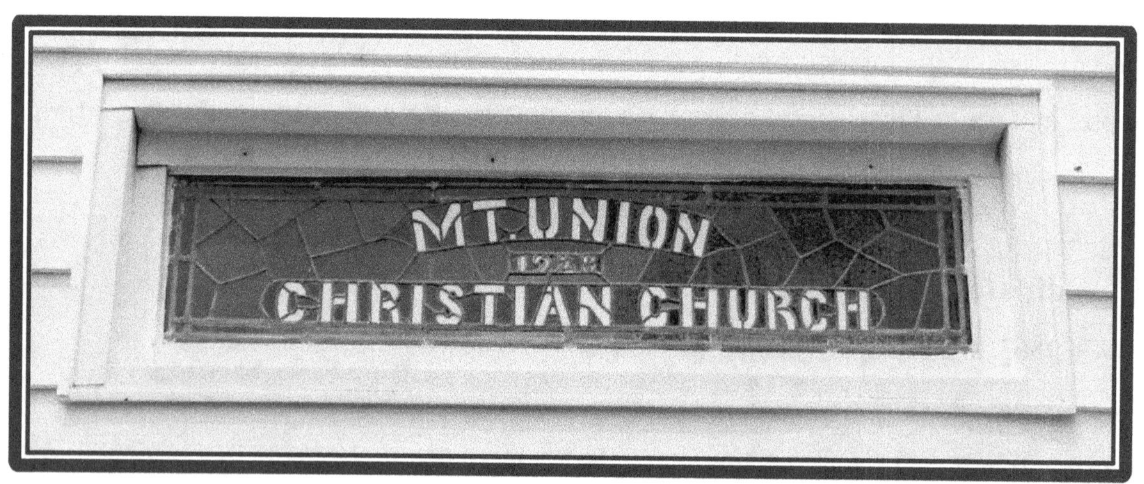

MT. UNION
1928
CHRISTIAN CHURCH

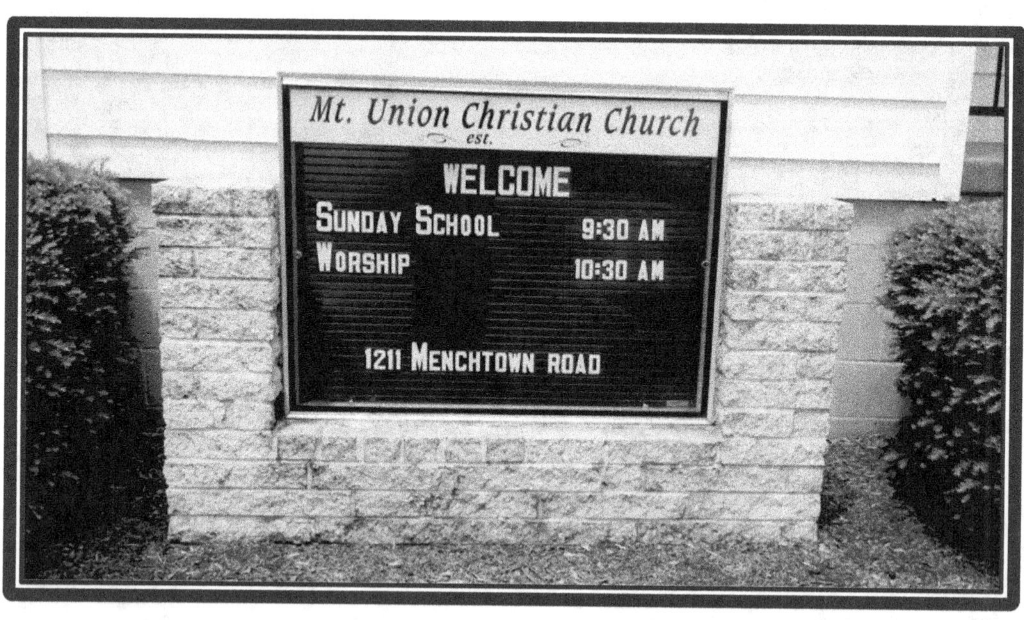

Mt. Union Christian Church
est.
WELCOME
SUNDAY SCHOOL   9:30 AM
WORSHIP   10:30 AM
1211 MENCHTOWN ROAD

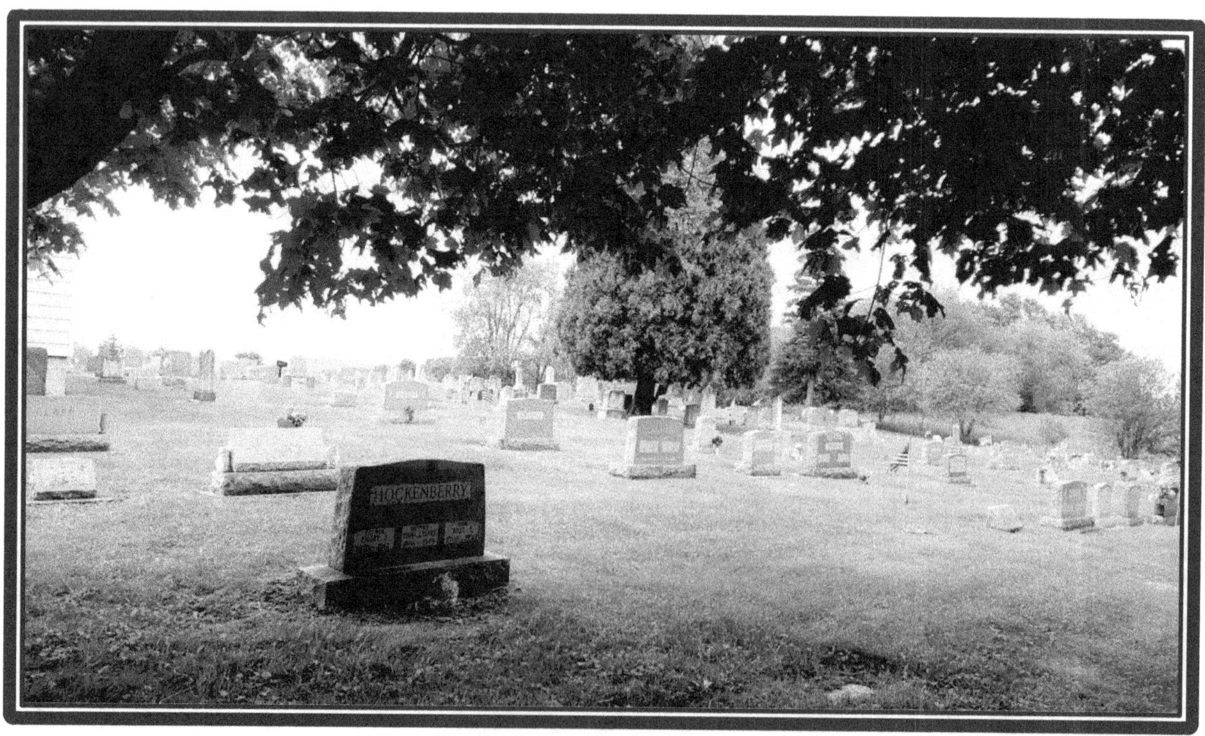

Cemetery List

NUMBER	NAMES/INSCRIPTIONS	BIRTH DATE	DEATH DATE	MISC. INFO.
1	EMORY J. HOCKENBERRY	JUNE 7, 1879	JUNE 6, 1961	TRIPLE STONE
2	EMMA I. (CLARK) HOCKENBERRY	NOV. 24, 1886	JAN. 21, 1949	
3	ROSS F. HOCKENBERRY	DEC. 21, 1908	MAR. 22, 1950	
4	OMER LEE PRICE TEC 5 US ARMY WORLD WAR II BRONZE STAR	AUG. 15, 1924	DEC. 27, 2008	
5	DORIS J. (MILLER) PRICE			
6	CAROLYN RUTH PRICE DAU. OF OMER AND DORIS PRICE	DEC. 26, 1953	DEC. 25, 1954	
7	PAUL E. PRICE	JULY 1, 1918	MAY 20, 1998	
8	CATHERINE M. (BROWN) PRICE	MAR. 2, 1924	APR. 2, 1999	
9	TAMMY P. (CHILDERS) BENTON	JUNE 15, 1968	MAY 4, 2009	
10	TINA MARIE CHILDERS	AUG. 18, 1965	APR. 15, 1997	
11	JAMES C. CALHOUN SGT E5 ARMY NATIONAL GUARD	MAY 28, 1936	JAN. 31, 2008	DOUBLE STONE
12	O. JANE (SHEIRER) CALHOUN	MAY 20, 1932		
13	FLOYD W. CALHOUN PFC US ARMY WORLD WAR II	NOV. 3, 1925	SEPT. 19, 1981	
14	DOROTHY M. (WINCK) CALHOUN	JULY 19, 1924	AUG. 20, 2002	
15	JACK M. CALHOUN US ARMY KOREA	JAN. 23, 1929	MAY 24, 2001	
16	HELEN JOYCE (PRICE) CHILDERS	AUG. 9, 1943	MAR. 28, 2015	
17	MARJORIE ELLEN SMITH	JAN. 24, 1929	SEPT. 28, 1946	
18	JOHN B. SMITH	MAR. 4, 1892	JAN. 24, 1972	DOUBLE STONE
19	JESSIE P. (BUSSARD) SMITH	JAN. 16, 1896	MAY 9, 1975	
20	J. HARVEY CALHOUN	AUG. 10, 1878	JAN. 13, 1954	DOUBLE STONE
21	ANNA M. (GRIMES) CALHOUN	JULY 13, 1887	MAR. 22, 1949	
22	ROY H. CALHOUN	FEB. 25, 1915	DEC. 23, 1966	
23	RALPH S. PRICE	JULY 7, 1911	APR. 20, 2004	DOUBLE STONE
24	GRACE A. (CALHOUN) PRICE	FEB. 13, 1914	JULY 16, 1967	
25	ROBERT WHITED	MAY 7, 1919	JAN. 22, 1988	DOUBLE STONE
26	BETTE (CALHOUN) WHITED	JUNE 24, 1923		

NUMBER	NAMES/INSCRIPTIONS	BIRTH DATE	DEATH DATE	MISC. INFO.
27	JOHN HENRY CALHOUN CPL US ARMY WORLD WAR II	JUNE 14, 1926	MAR. 19, 1994	
28	ESTHER O. (SEE) CALHOUN	JULY 1, 1928		
29	DEWEY LEADER	JULY 28, 1917	JUNE 22, 1999	
30	OMA MAXINE (MECK) LEADER	APR. 2, 1920	NOV. 12, 2011	
31	ZANE BRUCE LEADER SON OF DEWEY AND OMA LEADER	SEPT. 14, 1943	APR. 17, 1961	
32	EMORY C. HOCKENBERRY	JUNE 13, 1917	OCT. 8, 1993	
33	HELEN R. (MILLER) HOCKENBERRY	NOV. 26, 1918	JUNE 30, 2011	
34	JESSE CLARK	APR. 23, 1889	JULY 1, 1941	DOUBLE STONE
35	ETHEL (SMITH) CLARK	OCT. 2, 1898	NOV. 22, 1984	
36	WILBERT CLARK	MAY 1, 1925	SEPT. 10, 1932	
37	HAZEL EMMA SHIMER	MAR. 27, 1933	APR. 4, 1933	
38	HARRY W. SHIMER US ARMY WORLD WAR I	DEC. 26, 1893	FEB. 8, 1961	TRIPLE STONE
39	LAVERNE M. (DAVIS) SHIMER	NOV. 4, 1904	SEPT. 12, 1992	
40	FRANKLIN I. BROWN	JULY 3, 1896	JUNE 13, 1975	
41	MARGARET (JACKSON) BROWN	APR. 27, 1903	SEPT. 30, 1973	
42	JOSEPH EUGENE BROWN SON OF F. I. & I. M. BROWN	FEB. 20, 1936	MAY 27, 1936	DEATH CERTIFICATE LISTS DATES AS 1935.
43	CARL DUANE CHALFANT	MAY 2, 1959	MAY 26, 1963	
44	ROGER W. CHALFANT	MAR. 14, 1961	JUNE 24, 1961	
45	CAROL D. CHALFANT	APR. 13, 1963	APR. 25, 1963	
46	GERTRUDE GRACE CHALFANT	JULY 30, 1939	FEB. 25, 1941	MARKER HAS 1939-1941. DEATH CERTIFICATE HAS 1940-1942
47	CLAIR K. BRALLIER	FEB. 7, 1928	FEB. 3, 1994	DOUBLE STONE MARRIED APR. 11, 1952
48	DOLORES R. (PRICE) BRALLIER	APR. 11, 1933	APR. 14, 2012	
49	KENNETH CLAIR BRALLIER SON OF CLAIR AND DOLORES BRALLIER	JUNE 6, 1953	JAN. 25, 1954	
50	JOSEPH H. MILLER US ARMY WORLD WAR II	FEB. 9, 1925	SEPT. 11, 2015	DOUBLE STONE
51	HAZEL P. (PRICE) MILLER	MAR. 27, 1927		

NUMBER	NAMES/INSCRIPTIONS	BIRTH DATE	DEATH DATE	MISC. INFO.
52	GEORGE W. LEADER	JULY 9, 1906	NOV. 17, 1994	DOUBLE STONE
53	EVA M. (BUSSARD) LEADER	MAR. 13, 1907	JAN. 12, 1984	
54	GEORGE W. LEADER, JR.	MAR. 7, 1939	SEPT. 26, 2015	
55	LINDA SUE LEADER	MAY 27, 1946	AUG. 2, 1946	
56	DONALD D. LEADER, JR. SON OF DONALD AND CONNIE LEADER	JAN. 25, 1963	MAR. 23, 1963	
57	SANDRA JO LEADER DAU. OF JOHN W. & MILDRED LEADER	JULY 19, 1959	JULY 19, 1959	
58	JOHN C. CRISSEY CO. K. 208TH INF. PA. VOL. CIVIL WAR	NOV. 1, 1845	OCT. 4, 1911	DOUBLE STONE
59	SUSAN (HOCKENBERRY) CRISSEY	JAN. 25, 1852	OCT. 26, 1900	
60	WILLIAM G. SHAFFER	FEB. 2, 1875	FEB. 1, 1943	
61	SARAH E. (CLARK) SHAFFER	MAR. 3, 1879	NOV. 10, 1961	
62	INFANT SHOWALTERS SON OF A. B. AND L. J. SHOWALTERS		MAY 13, 1883	
63	SARAH J. (SPARKS) JAY	AUG. 2, 1869	MAY 18, 1897	DOUBLE STONE
64	DAVID W. JAY	APR. 3, 1860	DEC. 27, 1933	
65	GROVER C. JAY	AUG. 12, 1886	AUG. 19, 1886	TRIPLE STONE SONS OF D. W. & S. J. JAY
66	WALTER JAY	JULY 23, 1887	SEPT. 2, 1888	
67	ELMER JAY	MAR. 5, 1891	MAR. 31, 1891	
68	EDWARD JAY AGED 30 YEARS, 1 MONTH AND 4 DAYS		FEB. 4, 1895	TRIPLE STONE
69	JOHN JAY AGED 72 YEARS, 9 MONTHS AND 16 DAYS		OCT. 18, 1908	
70	LUCINDA (LEASURE) JAY WIFE OF JOHN JAY AGED 78 YEARS, 1 MONTH, AND 26 DAYS		AUG. 30, 1915	
71	ANNA LOUISE (JAY) SMITH	SEPT. 10, 1929	FEB. 28, 2016	
72	JAMES D. JAY	FEB. 2, 1931	MAY 19, 1945	
73	JOANNA (MILLER) JAY	SEPT. 12, 1910	DEC. 29, 2008	DOUBLE STONE
74	FLOYD JAY	JAN. 20, 1907	JAN. 10, 1995	
75	LILLIE J. (MCDANIEL) JACKSON WIFE OF J. U. JACKSON AGED 34 YEARS, 10 MONTHS AND 25 DAYS		SEPT. 19, 1895	

NUMBER	NAMES/INSCRIPTIONS	BIRTH DATE	DEATH DATE	MISC. INFO.
76	EDWARD C. JACKSON SON OF J. U. AND L. E. JACKSON AGED 4 MONTHS AND 24 DAYS		AUG. 11, 1887	
77	JOHN GILBERG AGED 72 YEARS		NOV. 7, 1898	
78	ELIZA A. (CLARK) GILBERG WIFE OF JOHN GILBERG AGED 72 YEARS, 6 MONTHS AND 27 DAYS		JAN. 12, 1914	DOUBLE STONE
79	MARY GILBERG AGED 71 YEARS AND 2 MONTHS		JULY 13, 1939	
80	JENNIE GILBERG DAU. OF JOHN AND ELIZA GILBERG AGED 30 YEARS, 7 MONTHS AND 10 DAYS		JULY 15, 1896	DOUBLE STONE
81	KENNETH GILBERG		APR. 23, 1913	
82	RUTH N. (SCOTT) CLITES	AUG. 26, 1921	AUG. 13, 1956	DOUBLE STONE
83	AMBROSE G. CLITES US ARMY WORLD WAR II	MAY 15, 1919	MAY 21, 1996	
84	RUTH SCOTT CLITES	1921	1956	DOUBLE STONE
85	MARY SCOTT	MAR. 3, 1938	MAR. 3, 1938	RUTH'S NAME IS ON TWO STONES, DATES ON BOTH STONES MATCH
86	JOHN LINDBURG SCOTT US ARMY WORLD WAR II	JAN. 31, 1928	APR. 5, 1983	
87	JOHN S. MORRIS	FEB. 13, 1820	FEB. 20, 1895	
88	SUSANNAH (BUSSARD) MORRIS WIFE OF JOHN S. MORRIS	JAN. 19, 1825	APR. 15, 1905	DOUBLE STONE
89	MARGARET LOGUE	1839	FEB. 2, 1934	HOUSEKEEPER FOR S. B. MORRIS
90	ELIZABETH (KEGG) MORRIS WIFE OF SAMUEL B. MORRIS	APR. 15, 1855	JAN. 1, 1933	DOUBLE STONE
91	SAMUEL B. MORRIS	APR. 26, 1853	SEPT. 10, 1932	
92	MARIA J. (WILLIAMS) MORRIS WIFE OF S. B. MORRIS AGED 27 YEARS, 3 MONTHS AND 18 DAYS		APR. 7, 1882	

NUMBER	NAMES/INSCRIPTIONS	BIRTH DATE	DEATH DATE	MISC. INFO.
93	LILLIE B. MORRIS AGED 3 MONTHS AND 1 DAY		FEB. 1, 1879	DOUBLE STONE CHILDREN OF S. B. & M. J. MORRIS
94	CARRIE A. MORRIS AGED 9 MONTHS AND 23 DAYS		AUG. 19, 1882	
95	MARY C. (KENNORD) MORRIS	JULY 20, 1849	JULY 20, 1921	DOUBLE STONE
96	ABRAM B. MORRIS	NOV. 26, 1849	MAR. 5, 1938	
97	ANNIE E. MORRIS DAU. OF A. B. & M. C. MORRIS AGED 26 YEARS, 9 MONTHS AND 7 DAYS		NOV. 10, 1910	
98	ELLA (FOOR) CLARK	JULY 11, 1867	APR. 6, 1936	TRIPLE STONE
99	GEORGE O. CLARK	JAN. 27, 1860	JUNE 30, 1935	
100	RACHEL (ROLLER) CLARK	1858	1894	
101	THOMAS CLARK SON OF G. O. & R. B. CLARK AGED 2 YEARS		NOV. 23, 1886	
102	MARY ELLEN CLARK	NOV. 24, 1884	NOV. 20, 1980	
103	INFANT WILLIAMS SON OF G. W. & M. J. WILLIAMS		MAY 30, 1893	
104	GEORGE W. WILLIAMS	JULY 6, 1838	MAR. 6, 1926	DOUBLE STONE
105	MARY J. (GRUBB) WILLIAMS WIFE OF GEORGE W. WILLIAMS	DEC. 4, 1849	FEB. 15, 1897	
106	CHARLES E. WILLIAMS	SEPT. 11, 1871	NOV. 2, 1951	DOUBLE STONE
107	FLORA E. (MCDANIEL) WILLIAMS WIFE OF CHARLES E. WILLIAMS	JULY 6, 1876	JAN. 11, 1931	
108	HIRAM E. HANN	SEPT. 22, 1870	MAR. 25, 1938	
109	LINNIE S. (WILLIAMS) HANN WIFE OF HIRAM E. HANN	NOV. 12, 1873	FEB. 19, 1950	
110	WILSON O'NEAL	AUG. 14, 1859	JAN. 9, 1936	
111	MATTIE P. (WILLIAMS) O'NEAL	AUG. 27, 1866	AUG. 24, 1933	
112	MARY ELIZABETH O'NEAL	AUG. 4, 1902	JAN. 31, 1904	

NUMBER	NAMES/INSCRIPTIONS	BIRTH DATE	DEATH DATE	MISC. INFO.
113	JOS. WILLIAMS CO. K. 208TH REG. PA. VOL. CIVIL WAR AGED 68 YEARS, 10 MONTHS AND 11 DAYS		JUNE 9, 1898	DOUBLE STONE
114	MARY (MCDANIEL) WILLIAMS WIFE OF JOS. WILLIAMS AGED 79 YEARS, 6 MONTHS AND 10 DAYS		MAY 19, 1914	
115	BARTON C. WILLIAMS AGED 20 YEARS, 3 MONTHS AND 7 DAYS		DEC. 5, 1879	
116	PHILLIP O'NEAL SON OF W. & M. O'NEAL AGED 1 YEAR, 4 MONTHS AND 5 DAYS		AUG. 9, 1888	
117	HARRY J. O'NEAL	OCT. 5, 1900	AUG. 2, 1923	
118	JOSEPH E. BUSSARD SON OF C. A. & M. J. BUSSARD	AUG. 31, 1885	SEPT. 13, 1886	
119	CLARENCE A. BUSSARD	MAY 12, 1860	APR. 3, 1905	
120	HATTIE VIOLA ZEMBOWER DAU. OF F. J. & C. J. ZEMBOWER AGED 3 YEARS, 3 MONTHS AND 29 DAYS		APR. 22, 1892	
121	CARRIE J. (MORTIMORE) ZEMBOWER	DEC. 19, 1863	MAR. 2, 1946	DOUBLE STONE
122	FRANK J. ZEMBOWER	SEPT. 29, 1866	AUG. 24, 1944	
123	JAMES A. CALHOUN SP4 US ARMY	MAY 15, 1937	JUNE 5, 2015	DOUBLE STONE
124	JANET B. (BOOR) CALHOUN	AUG. 11, 1938		
125	GERALDINE R. (KENNARD) CALHOUN DAU. OF GEORGE AND ADA (SHIPLEY) KENNARD	JULY 14, 1936		
126	DAVID EUGENE CALHOUN SON OF LLOYD AND ELDA (WILLIAMS) CALHOUN KOREA	NOV. 20, 1934	JULY 12, 2011	
127	ELIZABETH (ZEMBOWER) KEGG WIFE OF SEBASTIAN KEGG	DEC. 3, 1812	JAN. 26, 1900	

NUMBER	NAMES/INSCRIPTIONS	BIRTH DATE	DEATH DATE	MISC. INFO.
128	LEVI KEGG	NOV. 25, 1844	AUG. 1, 1921	DOUBLE STONE
129	EMILY (CALHOUN) KEGG WIFE OF LEVI KEGG	MAR. 11, 1850	NOV. 30, 1930	
130	STELLA E. WILT DAU. OF C. W. & A. E. WILT	OCT. 18, 1883	FEB. 5, 1889	
131	SARAH E. WILT DAU. OF C. W. & A. E. WILT	MAY 27, 1880	JUNE 19, 1880	
132	SARAH E. FEIGHT DAU. OF W. W. & L. FEIGHT AGED 7 YEARS, 6 MONTHS AND 29 DAYS		OCT. 30, 1884	
133	MARY L. FEIGHT DAU. OF W. W. & L. FEIGHT AGED 15 YEARS, 6 MONTHS AND 29 DAYS		FEB. 25, 1887	
134	VICTORIA FEIGHT DAU. OF W. W. & L. FEIGHT AGED 11 MONTHS AND 22 DAYS		APR. 18, 1887	
135	MINERVA FEIGHT DAU. OF W. W. & L. FEIGHT AGED 10 YEARS AND 27 DAYS		DEC. 20, 1888	
136	JOSIAH KISSEL AGED 72 YEARS, 8 MONTHS AND 4 DAYS	JUNE 11, 1854	FEB. 15, 1927	TRIPLE STONE
137	MARTHA (SHAW) KISSEL	APR. 2, 1859	SEPT. 18, 1940	
138	MARY ALICE KISSEL	JUNE 15, 1893	MAR. 27, 1922	
139	EDWARD KISSEL		MAR. 26, 1886	QUADRUPLE STONE CHILDREN OF J. & M. KISSEL
140	IRA W. KISSEL AGED 1 YEAR AND 19 DAYS		DEC. 8, 1888	
141	GEORGE W. KISSEL AGED 1 YEAR AND 6 MONTHS		APR. 2, 1893	
142	ORA V. KISSEL AGED 2 YEARS AND 5 DAYS		OCT. 26, 1898	
143	HENRY KISSEL CIVIL WAR AGED 67 YEARS, 4 MONTHS AND 10 DAYS		JUNE 30, 1886	
144	ELIZABETH (VEACH) KISSEL WIFE OF HENRY KISSEL	DEC. 18, 1820	MAR. 14, 1910	

NUMBER	NAMES/INSCRIPTIONS	BIRTH DATE	DEATH DATE	MISC. INFO.
145	BENJAMIN KISSEL CO. K. 208TH REGT. PA. VOL. CIVIL WAR	NOV. 4, 1843	MAR. 29, 1910	
146	WILLIAM J. KISSEL SON OF J. W. & M. J. KISSEL AGED 10 YEARS, 10 MONTHS AND 24 DAYS		JULY 2, 1880	
147	MARY E. KISSEL DAU. OF J. W. & M. J. KISSEL AGED 13 YEARS, 10 MONTHS AND 20 DAYS		SEPT. 4, 1897	
148	JOHN W. KISSEL 208TH REG. PA INF. CIVIL WAR	JULY 30, 1845	JAN. 7, 1911	
149	MARY JANE (LONG) KISSEL WIFE OF JOHN W. KISSEL	MAY 10, 1858	JULY 22, 1930	
150	STONE NO INSCRIPTION			
151	F. ADELLA KISSEL	MAR. 18, 1889	SEPT. 4, 1965	
152	ADAM SHUSS AGED 68 YEARS, 1 MONTH AND 28 DAYS CO. F. 56TH REGT. PA. VOL. CIVIL WAR		FEB. 10, 1897	DOUBLE STONE
153	ELIZABETH (CLINGERMAN) SHUSS WIFE OF ADAM SHUSS AGED 67 YEARS AND 27 DAYS		JAN. 21, 1897	
154	RAYMOND F. DEREMER SON OF J. F. & E. F. DEREMER AGED 6 MONTHS AND 14 DAYS		MAR. 8, 1897	
155	EMMA V. (SHUSS) DEREMER WIFE OF J. FRANK DEREMER AGED 32 YEARS, 3 MONTHS AND 2 DAYS		JAN. 16, 1900	DOUBLE STONE
156	EMELINE PERRIN AGED 49 YEARS, 6 MONTHS AND 10 DAYS		SEPT. 10, 1898	
157	LOUISA J. PERRIN WIFE OF T. PERRIN AGED 63 YEARS AND 9 MONTHS		JAN. 12, 1884	

NUMBER	NAMES/INSCRIPTIONS	BIRTH DATE	DEATH DATE	MISC. INFO.
158	ELISA CLARK AGED 85 YEARS, 3 MONTHS AND 19 DAYS		OCT. 27, 1890	
159	ESTHER (HELY) CLARK WIFE OF ELISA CLARK AGED 70 YEARS AND 3 MONTHS		MAR. 4, 1880	
160	HARRIET (CLARK) MILLS WIFE OF LEWIS MILLS	JAN. 18, 1856	JUNE 8, 1881	
161	CLEVELAND LEADER SON OF G. W. & M. LEADER AGED 5 MONTHS AND 10 DAYS		MAR. 13, 1885	
162	RAYMOND H. LEADER SON OF G. W. & M. LEADER	APR. 30, 1893	MAR. 6, 1898	
163	VIRGIN O. LEADER DAU. OF G. W. & M. LEADER	MAR. 16, 1889	MAR. 25, 1898	
164	JOHN L. LEADER SON OF GEORGE W. & MARGARET LEADER	MAR. 17, 1888	FEB. 12, 1920	
165	GEORGE W. LEADER, JR. AGED 85 YEARS, 9 MONTHS AND 20 DAYS CO. F. 8TH REG. PA RES. CIVIL WAR	APR. 9, 1839	JAN. 29, 1925	DOUBLE STONE
166	MARGARET (SLEIGHTER) LEADER WIFE OF GEORGE W. LEADER, JR.	JUNE 8, 1848	MAY 25, 1924	
167	ROCKSANNAH WELCH		MAR. 15, 1884	
168	ANDREW J. CALHOUN	DEC. 2, 1861	MAY 14, 1889	
169	MARY (MCDANIEL) KEGG CALHOUN	OCT. 1, 1862	NOV. 29, 1951	TRIPLE STONE
170	CHESTER D. CALHOUN	NOV. 27, 1885	MAR. 31, 1887	
171	ELIZA MCDANIEL WIFE OF JOHN MCDANIEL AGED 74 YEARS AND 2 MONTHS		MAY 8, 1883	
172	MARY S. CRAWFORD DAU. OF W. & H. C.CRAWFORD AGED 1 YEAR, 2 MONTHS AND 23 DAYS		JUNE 27, 1884	
173	JAMES E. GORDON SON OF W. S. & L. B. GORDON AGED 9 MONTHS AND 12 DAYS		JAN. 16, 1880	

NUMBER	NAMES/INSCRIPTIONS	BIRTH DATE	DEATH DATE	MISC. INFO.
174	SAMUEL ORVILLE GORDON PVT. CO. H. 17TH BN I.R. & T.C. US ARMY WORLD WAR I	MAR. 15, 1895	NOV. 22, 1934	
175	W. SCOTT GORDON	JUNE 2, 1855	JAN. 8, 1945	DOUBLE STONE
176	LAURA A. (CLARK) GORDON	JULY 27, 1861	MAR. 5, 1941	
177	PHILIP RITCHEY	MAY 18, 1818	OCT. 23, 1887	DOUBLE STONE
178	MARY (MIXEL) RITCHEY	APR. 12, 1820	JUNE 24, 1898	
179	SARA (RITCHEY) KARNS	NOV. 22, 1846	JUNE 1909	
180	JACOB RITCHEY	JULY 12, 1859	MAY 15, 1923	DOUBLE STONE
181	MARY A. (CLARK) RITCHEY	1865	1923	
182	JOHN R. RITCHEY SON OF J. R. & M. A. RITCHEY	MAR. 10, 1892	DEC. 20, 1900	
183	EDITH M. RITCHEY DAU. OF J. R. & M. A. RITCHEY	JULY 11, 1900	JULY 11, 1900	
184	ETHAL E. RITCHEY DAU. OF J. R. & M. A. RITCHEY	AUG. 7, 1899	MAY 14, 1900	
185	HENRY H. LEADER CO. H. 2ND REGT. PA ARTILLERY CIVIL WAR	JUNE 2, 1843	AUG. 3, 1893	DOUBLE STONE
186	CATHERINE (AKINSON) LEADER WIFE OF DAVID LEADER AGED ABOUT 90 YEARS		APR. 10, 1900	
187	INFANT WILLIAMS SON OF J. H. & M. B. WILLIAMS AGED 7 DAYS		AUG. 27, 1888	
188	RUTH WILLIAMS DAU. OF J. H. & M. B. WILLIAMS	1895	1898	
189	JAMES H. WILLIAMS	FEB. 13, 1856	FEB. 8, 1930	
190	MINNIE B. (AKERS) WILLIAMS WIFE OF J. H. WILLIAMS	DEC. 20, 1863	JAN. 19, 1923	
191	SOLOMON WILLIAMS	NOV. 7, 1803	NOV. 3, 1878	DOUBLE STONE
192	HANNAH (VEATCH) WILLIAMS WIFE OF SOLOMON WILLIAMS	AUG. 2, 1825	AUG. 13, 1902	
193	EDWIN S. WILLIAMS SON OF SOLOMON AND HANNAH WILLIAMS	1868	1879	

NUMBER	NAMES/INSCRIPTIONS	BIRTH DATE	DEATH DATE	MISC. INFO.
194	HANNAH (ZEMBOWER) WILLIAMS WIFE OF W. B. WILLIAMS AGED 24 YEARS, 6 MONTHS AND 29 DAYS		JULY 5, 1881	
195	MOLLIE J. WEAVERLING WIFE OF S. W. WEAVERLING AGED 44 YEARS AND 21 DAYS		JAN. 7, 1900	
196	ELLA WEAVERLING WIFE OF S. W. WEAVERLING AGED 24 YEARS, 3 MONTHS AND 6 DAYS		APR. 1, 1887	
197	DESSIE M. WEAVERLING DAU. OF S. W. & E. WEAVERLING		JUNE 29, 1889	
198	GEORGE W. KEGG AGED 37 YEARS, 7 MONTHS AND 2 DAYS		OCT. 15, 1895	
199	MARY E. (WILLIAMS) KEGG WIFE OF GEORGE W. KEGG AGED 33 YEARS, 6 MONTHS AND 14 DAYS		MAR. 22, 1891	
200	ALBERT CALHOUN	AUG. 19, 1881	DEC. 22, 1962	DOUBLE STONE
201	EDNA W. (KEGG) CALHOUN	JAN. 1, 1881	JUNE 14, 1961	
202	GRANT H. DECKER SON OF A. H. & C. F. DECKER			STONE IS NOT READABLE. PREVIOUS READ WAS 1973
203	FRANCES E. DECKER DAU. OF A. H. & C. F. DECKER	JAN. 27, 1881	NOV. 24, 1903	
204	STONE NO INSCRIPTION			
205	A. H. DECKER	SEPT. 25, 1856	NOV. 3, 1924	
206	CATHERINE (FISHER) DECKER WIFE OF A. H. DECKER	NOV. 25, 1850	APR. 22, 1939	

NUMBER	NAMES/INSCRIPTIONS	BIRTH DATE	DEATH DATE	MISC. INFO.
207	SIMON S. BUSSARD AGED 74 YEARS, 7 MONTHS AND 13 DAYS CO. H. 99TH REGT. P. V. CIVIL WAR		DEC. 14, 1916	DOUBLE STONE
208	REBECCA J. (KEGG) BUSSARD WIFE OF SIMON S. BUSSARD AGED 66 YEARS, 9 MONTHS AND 24 DAYS		APR. 20, 1908	
209	EDWARD J. STECKMAN SON OF A. & M. STECKMAN	JULY 6, 1895	SEPT. 8, 1895	
210	ALBERT STECKMAN AGED 86 YEARS, 1 MONTH AND 25 DAYS		APR. 27, 1950	DOUBLE STONE
211	MARTHA (BENNETT) STECKMAN WIFE OF ALBERT STECKMAN AGED 42 YEARS, 8 MONTHS AND 17 DAYS		FEB. 3, 1909	
212	HENRY BENNETT CO. I. 91ST REG. P. V. CIVIL WAR	AUG. 20, 1835	JAN. 13, 1919	DOUBLE STONE
213	ANN M. (PERDEW) BENNETT WIFE OF HENRY BENNETT	APR. 9, 1838	OCT. 11, 1906	
214	MALINDA BENNETT DAU. OF H. & A. M. BENNETT AGED 16 YEARS, 3 MONTHS AND 9 DAYS		APR. 25, 1876	
215	HOWARD M. MORTIMORE SON OF A. & M. C. MORTIMORE		NOV. 24, 1872	
216	OLIVER ZEMBOWER SON OF J. & E. ZEMBOWER AGED 9 YEARS, 11 MONTHS AND 18 DAYS		APR. 1861	
217	EMMA ZEMBOWER DAU. OF J. & E. ZEMBOWER AGED 3 MONTHS AND 13 DAYS		NOV. 4, 1861	

NUMBER	NAMES/INSCRIPTIONS	BIRTH DATE	DEATH DATE	MISC. INFO.
218	GEORGE M. ZEMBOWER SON OF J. & E. ZEMBOWER AGED 1 MONTH AND 10 DAYS		MAY 22, 1861	
219	JOSIAH ZEMBOWER CO. G 186TH REGT. PA INF. CIVIL WAR	JUNE 15, 1828	JULY 27, 1913	DOUBLE STONE
220	ELIZA (BOTTENFIELD) ZEMBOWER WIFE OF JOSIAH ZEMBOWER	AUG. 5, 1833	JAN. 25, 1907	
221	CLARA EVELYN WILLIAMS	DEC. 9, 1902	JULY 2, 1903	
222	JOHN ZEMBOWER AGED 77 YEARS		APR. 15, 1862	
223	ELIZABETH (FILLER) ZEMBOWER AGED 88 YEARS		FEB. 20, 1868	TRIPLE STONE
224	REBECCA ZEMBOWER AGED 47 YEARS		OCT. 20, 1868	
225	JAMES ZEMBOWER AGED 63 YEARS		APR. 9, 1885	
226	WALTER R. ZEMBOWER SON OF W. A. & J. E. ZEMBOWER AGED 2 MONTHS AND 11 DAYS		MAY 19, 1887	
227	ELGIE M. ZEMBOWER DAU. OF W. A. & J. E. ZEMBOWER AGED 1 MONTH AND 3 DAYS		MAR. 19, 1883	TRIPLE STONE
228	MURRY E. ZEMBOWER SON OF W. A. & J. E. ZEMBOWER AGED 10 YEARS, 6 MONTHS AND 2 DAYS		OCT. 14, 1891	
229	JUDITH E. (O'NEAL) ZEMBOWER WIFE OF W. A. ZEMBOWER AGED 45 YEARS AND 20 DAYS		FEB. 26, 1905	
230	SUSAN MARGARET (MCDANIEL) WILLIAMS WIFE OF ALBERT E. WILLIAMS AGED 33 YEARS, 8 MONTHS AND 15 DAYS		OCT. 28, 1895	

NUMBER	NAMES/INSCRIPTIONS	BIRTH DATE	DEATH DATE	MISC. INFO.
231	ROY RAYMOND WILLIAMS SON OF A. E. & S. M. WILLIAMS AGED 6 MONTHS AND 12 DAYS		JUNE 2, 1895	THERE ARE SIX (6) PEOPLE LISTED ON THIS TOMBSTONE.
232	INFANT WILLIAMS SON OF A. E. & S. M. WILLIAMS		JULY 29, 1880	
233	ALBERT E. WILLIAMS AGED 43 YEARS, 1 MONTH AND 1 DAY		MAR. 21, 1898	
234	MARY L. WILLIAMS DAU. OF A. E. & S. M. WILLIAMS AGED 11 YEARS, 8 MONTHS AND 10 DAYS		APR. 15, 1897	
235	CLIFFORD E. WILLIAMS SON OF A. E. & S. M. WILLIAMS AGED 7 YEARS, 7 MONTHS AND 29 DAYS		NOV. 20, 1899	
236	ASA WILLIAMS AGED 18 YEARS	APR. 1, 1883	JAN. 18, 1902	
237	MYRA V. WILLIAMS COBLER	NOV. 1887	OCT. 1912	
238	LLOYD H. CALHOUN	MAR. 29, 1907	APR. 18, 1996	DOUBLE STONE
239	ELDA W. (WILLIAMS) CALHOUN	NOV. 20, 1904	AUG. 17, 1994	
240	ROSS WILSON MCDANIEL	SEPT. 21, 1879	MAY 27, 1961	DOUBLE STONE
241	ROSIE (SOLLENBERGER) MCDANIEL	MAY 25, 1881	JULY 31, 1963	
242	ORVILE R. MILLER	FEB. 3, 1916	JAN. 1, 1996	DOUBLE STONE
243	MILDRED A. (SNOW) MILLER	MAY 3, 1920	DEC. 18, 2005	
244	TROY M. MILLER	APR. 9, 1970	JUNE 14, 1999	
245	PAUL W. MILLER	OCT. 30, 1953	OCT. 21, 2005	
246	DAVID L. CLARK	FEB. 13, 1856	JAN. 7, 1930	DOUBLE STONE
247	RACHEL C. (BEQUEATH) CLARK	MAR. 20, 1850	SEPT. 19, 1929	
248	E. WATSON BARTON	MAY 10, 1879	MAR. 9, 1926	DOUBLE STONE
249	ETTIE L. (BUSSARD) BARTON WIFE OF E. WATSON BARTON	OCT. 15, 1872	SEPT. 7, 1909	
250	NELLIE MAY BARTON DAU. OF E. WATSON AND ETTIE L. BARTON	MAY 8, 1909	AUG. 14, 1909	
251	DAISY (BARTON) AKERS	NOV. 18, 1902	FEB. 24, 1979	

NUMBER	NAMES/INSCRIPTIONS	BIRTH DATE	DEATH DATE	MISC. INFO.
252	SAMUEL IRONS AGED ABOUT 72 YEARS		NOV. 17, 1902	DOUBLE STONE NO DATES ON ELIZABETH'S STONE. INFO IS FROM DEATH CERTIFICATE.
253	ELIZABATH (SMITH) IRONS WIFE OF SAMUEL IRONS AGED ABOUT 80 YEARS		NOV. 15, 1914	
254	ANNIE L. (IRONS) CLARK WIFE OF NELSON CLARK	JUNE 26, 1863	APR. 7, 1893	
255	MARY LIZZIE CLARK DAU. OF N. & A. L. CLARK	JUNE 18, 1886	MAR. 24, 1887	
256	CHRISTOPHER P. CALHOUN, M.D. CO. F. 138TH REGT. PA VOL. CIVIL WAR	JULY 9, 1842	MAY 18, 1902	
257	JOHN C. CALHOUN	JULY 2, 1816	FEB. 4, 1892	
258	ANN (CALHOUN) FRAZEY AGED 84 YEARS, 1 MONTH, 5 DAYS		SEPT. 10, 1886	
259	MARY CALHOUN DAU. OF J. C. & E. CALHOUN AGED 27 YEARS, 8 MONTHS AND 23 DAYS		SEPT. 18, 1883	
260	WILLIAM J. BUSSARD	JAN. 3, 1868	DEC. 21, 1957	
261	AMANDA C. (REDINGER) BUSSARD	APR. 17, 1869	APR. 14, 1949	DOUBLE STONE
262	CARRIE A. BUSSARD	DEC. 15, 1895	JAN. 26, 1896	
263	ELSIE M. MCDANIEL DAU. OF O. & M. MCDANIEL AGED 4 YEARS, 3 MONTHS AND 16 DAYS		FEB. 22, 1887	
264	MIRIAM (CALHOUN) MCDANIEL WIFE OF OLIVER MCDANIEL AGED 51 YEARS, 3 MONTHS AND 14 DAYS		DEC. 26, 1898	
265	OLIVER MCDANIEL CO. K. 78TH REGT. PA INF. CIVIL WAR	DEC. 26, 1840	JAN. 2, 1908	
266	GEORGE W. BUSSARD	AUG. 11, 1864	JUNE 15, 1926	DOUBLE STONE
267	OCIE E. (WILLIAMS) BUSSARD	OCT. 26, 1868	SEPT. 14, 1949	
268	INFANT DAUGHTER BUSSARD		1893	
269	INFANT SON BUSSARD		1897	
270	STONE NO INSCRIPTION			
271	STONE NO INSCRIPTION			

NUMBER	NAMES/INSCRIPTIONS	BIRTH DATE	DEATH DATE	MISC. INFO.
272	DAVID E. CALHOUN	AUG. 12, 1885	JUNE 1, 1956	
273	MYRTLE M. (HOCKENBERRY) CALHOUN	FEB. 14, 1887	JUNE 23, 1975	DOUBLE STONE
274	GLENN D. CALHOUN SON OF D. E. & M. M. CALHOUN	JUNE 27, 1914	JULY 21, 1935	
275	SOLOMON W. KEGG	NOV. 24, 1846	MAY 21, 1927	
276	AMANDA (WILLIAMS) KEGG WIFE OF SOLOMON KEGG	SEPT. 12, 1848	DEC. 22, 1934	DOUBLE STONE
277	REV. JOHN S. KEGG	JUNE 29, 1881	SEPT. 26, 1944	
278	B. FLORENCE (SHAW) KEGG	OCT. 13, 1885	JUNE 17, 1979	DOUBLE STONE
279	GEORGE E. SMITH AGED 70 YEARS	1874	OCT. 21, 1944	
280	ETTA V. (REDINGER) SMITH	SEPT. 1878	1965	DOUBLE STONE
281	VERA P. SMITH	FEB. 22, 1911	JAN. 31, 1967	
282	UNREADABLE SMALL LAMB STONE			APPEARS TO BE THE NAME JOHN WITH A DATE OF AUGUST OR OCTOBER 11.
283	CARRIE M. (KEGG) MILLIN WIFE OF A. W. MILLIN	AUG. 13, 1872	MAY 22, 1917	
284	SAMUEL C. LAYTON	JUNE 9, 1868	MAY 5, 1954	
285	MINNIE E. (KEGG) LAYTON	NOV. 14, 1870	FEB. 1, 1907	DOUBLE STONE
286	EMILY M. LAYTON DAU. OF S. C. & M. E. LAYTON	OCT. 13, 1902	DEC. 3, 1924	
287	EDITH GRACE LAYTON DAU. OF S. C. & M. E. LAYTON	SEPT. 19, 1897	OCT. 30, 1904	
288	ELMER VAUGHN LAYTON SON OF S. C. & M. E. LAYTON	JAN. 25, 1901	SEPT. 29, 1901	
289	DAVID C. CALHOUN CO. C. 82ND REGT. PA INF. CIVIL WAR	APR. 6, 1829	JUNE 12, 1900	
290	LUCINDA (KEGG) CALHOUN AGED 77 YEARS, 3 MONTHS AND 11 DAYS	NOV. 9, 1839	FEB. 20, 1917	
291	JOHN H. CALHOUN	JULY 13, 1860	JUNE 27, 1903	
292	MYRTLE C. CALHOUN AGED 29 YEARS, 2 MONTHS AND 1 DAY	JAN. 23, 1880	MAR. 24, 1909	
293	SARA ADA CALHOUN	MAR. 28, 1882	MAR. 25, 1931	

NUMBER	NAMES/INSCRIPTIONS	BIRTH DATE	DEATH DATE	MISC. INFO.
294	JOHN C. STREIGHT	JUNE 15, 1862	APR. 11, 1932	DOUBLE STONE
295	MARY A. (PEE) STREIGHT WIFE OF JOHN C. STREIGHT	JUNE 17, 1864	JUNE 5, 1943	
296	ROSA E. (BUSSARD) STREIGHT WIFE OF J. C. STREIGHT AGED 32 YEARS, 8 MONTHS AND 23 DAYS		AUG. 6, 1902	QUADRUPLE STONE
297	ILA R. STREIGHT AGED 10 DAYS		SEPT. 22, 1899	
298	INAH M. STREIGHT AGED 10 DAYS		DEC. 12, 1901	
299	EDITH E. STREIGHT AGED 1 YEAR, 4 MONTHS AND 14 DAYS		APR. 27, 1902	
300	JOHN NELSON WILLIAMS	JUNE 21, 1858	DEC. 7, 1919	DOUBLE STONE
301	SARAH (MORGART) WILLIAMS	AUG. 2, 1860	JULY 23, 1935	
302	ESTELLA MAY WILLIAMS DAU. OF J. N. & SARAH E. WILLIAMS AGED 22 YEARS, 4 MONTHS AND 28 DAYS		JAN. 3, 1904	
303	SARAH ELLEN JAY DAU. OF D. & M. JAY			NO DATES ON STONE.
304	LISA MARIE WHISEL INFANT	1960	1960	
305	C. MARIE (WILLIAMS) JAY GRUBB	SEPT. 9, 1900	DEC. 27, 1975	DOUBLE STONE CATHERINE WAS MARRIED A SECOND TIME TO LUTHER H. GRUBB
306	DEWEY JAY	APR. 19, 1899	FEB. 17, 1944	
307	FRANK H. O'NEAL	OCT. 1866	SEPT. 1951	TRIPLE STONE
308	BERTIE E. (WILLIAMS) O'NEAL	NOV. 18, 1874	MAR. 19, 1945	
309	HENRY W. O'NEAL	AUG. 1899	MAR. 1920	
310	FRANK H. PRICE	JULY 18, 1881	JAN. 5, 1963	DOUBLE STONE
311	ETHEL M. (MORRIS) PRICE	JULY 7, 1889	DEC. 17, 1960	
312	INFANT SON PRICE SON OF F. H. & E. M. PRICE		OCT. 15, 1916	
313	PERCY T. DUVALL	MAR. 8, 1911	AUG. 11, 1987	DOUBLE STONE
314	THEORA C. (MORSE) DUVALL	JAN. 9, 1914	APR. 12, 2003	
315	JOHN E. MORSE	MAY 2, 1879	JAN. 11, 1965	DOUBLE STONE
316	MARY ETTA (SMITH) MORSE	MAR. 19, 1882	JULY 30, 1956	
317	INFANTS MORSE DAUGHTERS OF J. E. & M. E. MORSE		MAY 16, 1911	

NUMBER	NAMES/INSCRIPTIONS	BIRTH DATE	DEATH DATE	MISC. INFO.
318	JAMES CARROLL LEE PVT US ARMY WORLD WAR I	MAY 20, 1898	OCT. 17, 1920	
319	RAYMOND ELVIN LEE PVT CO. A. 29TH INF. 33RD DIV. US ARMY WORLD WAR I	JULY 13, 1895	JULY 6, 1925	
320	LAURA (MCDANIEL) SLONAKER LEE	NOV. 29, 1870	APR. 26, 1953	
321	WILSON MCDANIEL	JAN. 24, 1831	FEB. 22, 1913	DOUBLE STONE
322	ALCINDA (WILLIAMS) MCDANIEL	AUG. 22, 1840	MAR. 19, 1917	
323	DAVID H. LEADER	FEB. 22, 1874	JULY 28, 1946	DOUBLE STONE
324	ROSIE (BUSSARD) LEADER	FEB. 11, 1882	FEB. 27, 1954	
325	OLIVE LEADER DAU. OF D. H. & R. R. LEADER	JAN. 8, 1903	FEB. 15, 1906	
326	J. ELSWORTH LEADER SON OF DAVID & ROSIE LEADER	NOV. 29, 1910	AUG. 2, 1943	
327	JOHN E. MELLOTT	JULY 18, 1878	FEB. 22, 1967	
328	MARY E. (DIBERT) MELLOTT WIFE OF JOHN MELLOTT	FEB. 18, 1860	APR. 17, 1939	
329	THOMAS DIBERT	NOV. 12, 1832	MAY 13, 1911	
330	SARAH (SHUSS) DIBERT WIFE OF THOMAS DIBERT	AUG. 1, 1832	MAY 24, 1905	
331	W. BRUCE STEACH	MAR. 26, 1899	APR. 26, 1962	DOUBLE STONE
332	OPHA E. (KARNS) STEACH	JUNE 21, 1899	FEB. 6, 1969	
333	HAROLD W. STEACH	FEB. 12, 1919	AUG. 13, 1940	
334	HAZEL G. STEACH	MAY 13, 1926	MAR. 7, 1940	
335	IRA D. COOPER	JULY 23, 1887	NO DATE	DOUBLE STONE
336	M. REBA (WILLIAMS) COOPER	JULY 21, 1890	OCT. 26, 1918	
337	KATHRYN M. COOPER RAISED BY CHARLES & ELVA SLEIGHTER	SEPT. 26, 1916	JULY 14, 1994	
338	WALTER G. BUSSARD	FEB. 16, 1908	MAY 16, 1984	DOUBLE STONE
339	ARLENE (ANDREWS) BUSSARD	JUNE 10, 1912	FEB. 23, 1985	
340	FRANK BUSSARD	JULY 3, 1910	AUG. 13, 1993	DOUBLE STONE
341	ANNA (RITCHEY) BUSSARD	MAR. 22, 1915	JULY 27, 1995	
342	LESTER H. DECKER	NOV. 6, 1887	JAN. 26, 1966	
343	MABEL R. (WIGFIELD) DECKER	APR. 28, 1893	OCT. 14, 1934	
344	JOHN H. DECKER	SEPT. 14, 1911	SEPT. 14, 1911	DOUBLE STONE
345	PEARL A. DECKER	FEB. 14, 1912	SEPT. 25, 1914	

NUMBER	NAMES/INSCRIPTIONS	BIRTH DATE	DEATH DATE	MISC. INFO.
346	GEORGE CLARK	JUNE 18, 1850	AUG. 23, 1922	DOUBLE STONE
347	CATHARINE D. (ROLLER) CLARK	FEB. 3, 1849	JULY 10, 1926	
348	SARAH (VEACH) MCDANIEL WIFE OF JAMES MCDANIEL AGED 86 YEARS, 9 MONTHS AND 12 DAYS	AUG. 22, 1823	MAY 4, 1910	
349	JACOB E. MELLOTT			DOUBLE STONE
350	SUSAN (COOPER) MELLOTT WIFE OF JACOB E. MELLOTT AGED 59 YEARS, 2 MONTHS AND 29 DAYS	DEC. 24, 1849	MAR. 23, 1909	
351	CHARLES A. GORDON	DEC. 8, 1880	NOV. 17, 1964	
352	SARAH C. (MILLS) GORDON WIFE OF CHARLES GORDON	JAN. 19, 1886	OCT. 8, 1909	
353	EDGAR R. GORDON SON OF C. A. & S. C. GORDON	MAR. 28, 1908	JULY 22, 1917	
354	SHERRY ANN CALHOUN	OCT. 3, 1951	JUNE 8, 1954	DOUBLE STONE CHILDREN OF P. C. & C. J. CALHOUN
355	TERRY LEE CALHOUN SON OF P. C. & C. J. CALHOUN	OCT. 28, 1953	DEC. 22, 1953	
356	EDWARD W. CALHOUN	SEPT. 30, 1888	FEB. 19, 1978	DOUBLE STONE
357	CARRIE (BOWEN) CALHOUN	SEPT. 20, 1891	MAY 19, 1983	
358	PALMER STRATTON CALHOUN	AUG. 29, 1929	MAY 25, 2017	
359	STONE INSCRIBED SAMIKOS			
360	FRANK ENGLAND AGED 27 YEARS, 4 MONTHS AND 20 DAYS		JULY 18, 1917	DOUBLE STONE
361	WALTER H. ENGLAND		MAY 1, 1915	
362	MAMIE (SMITH) STEACH	NOV. 1, 1890	MAR. 4, 1960	DOUBLE STONE
363	MARIAM (STEACH) SIPES	MAR. 20, 1925	OCT. 20, 1957	
364	ELSIE VIOLA STEACH	SEPT. 20, 1913	JUNE 17, 1934	TRIPLE STONE
365	EDWARD CHARLES STEACH	NOV. 17, 1920	SEPT. 18, 1925	
366	JOSEPH HOWARD STEACH	NOV. 8, 1922	JUNE 4, 1927	
367	ABRAM S. BUSSARD	DEC. 7, 1845	MAY 2, 1907	
368	SUSAN A. (RITCHEY) BUSSARD	JULY 14, 1848	MAR. 22, 1920	

NUMBER	NAMES/INSCRIPTIONS	BIRTH DATE	DEATH DATE	MISC. INFO.
369	MARY E. (BUSSARD) STEACH	MAR. 13, 1871	JULY 13, 1935	TRIPLE STONE
370	SAMUEL S. STEACH	AUG. 12, 1860	SEPT. 25, 1931	
371	GRANT U. STEACH	DEC. 22, 1892	APR. 1, 1959	
372	OPHELIA (PRICE) KEGG	SEPT. 16, 1886	OCT. 2, 1931	QUADRUPLE STONE
373	STANLEY KEGG	OCT. 4, 1885	JUNE 29, 1946	
374	MARY LOIS KEGG	OCT. 22, 1923	DEC. 28, 1924	
375	INFANT KEGG	FEB. 2, 1919	FEB. 14, 1920	
376	HARRY E. COUGHENOUR	MAR. 5, 1883	NOV. 21, 1968	DOUBLE STONE
377	LILLIE V. (PRICE) COUGHENOUR	SEPT. 30, 1884	JAN. 14, 1917	
378	RUSSELL P. COUGHENOUR	MAR. 10, 1909	APR. 7, 1988	
379	JOHN C. VEATCH CO. A. 11TH REGT. P. V. I. CIVIL WAR	OCT. 13, 1839	MAY 29, 1911	
380	ADALINE (MILLER) VEATCH WIFE OF JOHN C. VEATCH	NOV. 18, 1854	SEPT. 12, 1914	DEATH CERTIFICATE LISTS DATE OF DEATH AS SEPT. 11
381	GEORGE O. CALHOUN	NOV. 10, 1886	JULY 25, 1971	
382	LILLIE V. (BUSSARD) CALHOUN	DEC. 3, 1887	JULY 13, 1974	
383	EARL E. CALHOUN SGT SQ A-1 ARMY AIR FORCE WORLD WAR II	JULY 11, 1926	FEB. 25, 1972	
384	JOHN EDWIN CALHOUN SON OF GEO. & LILLIE V. CALHOUN	JULY 2, 1924	AUG. 31, 1925	
385	PHILIP A. WIGFIELD	JUNE 28, 1875	MAY 14, 1920	
386	MARTHA R. (CALHOUN) WIGFIELD	MAY 18, 1874	MAY 22, 1934	2ND MARRIAGE TO WEICHT
387	LIZZIE M. VAN HORN	MAR. 1, 1874	NOV. 28, 1949	
388	JOHN M. VAN HORN CO. C. 133RD REGT. PA. INF. CIVIL WAR	MAR. 28, 1845	JAN. 31, 1921	DOUBLE STONE
389	CATHARINE (WEEKS) VAN HORN	SEPT. 14, 1846	MAR. 4, 1931	
390	LUTHER W. DAVIS	AUG. 7, 1918	JUNE 20, 1942	
391	SADIE M. (MELLOTT) WEAVERLING	AUG. 25, 1880	JAN. 26, 1973	THERE ARE FIVE (5) PEOPLE LISTED ON THIS STONE.
392	SCOTT W. WEAVERLING	SEPT. 11, 1861	APR. 21, 1940	
393	MARGRIE E. WEAVERLING	FEB. 13, 1909	AUG. 21, 1910	
394	AMOS P. WEAVERLING	MAY 21, 1911	AUG. 3, 1912	
395	ANNIE S. WEAVERLING	1915	1926	

NUMBER	NAMES/INSCRIPTIONS	BIRTH DATE	DEATH DATE	MISC. INFO.
396	JENNIE (MCDANIEL) JACKSON WIFE OF JOHN S. JACKSON	APR. 10, 1872	SEPT. 16, 1915	
397	J. RITNER FOOR	MAR. 11, 1869	AUG. 21, 1917	DOUBLE STONE
398	DORA M. (LEADER) FOOR WIFE OF J. RITNER FOOR	MAY 1, 1868	APR. 24, 1948	
399	GEORGE W. FOOR	JUNE 1, 1906	APR. 5, 1974	
400	STONE INSCRIBED SALYARDS			
401	CHARLES H. PEPPLE	APR. 30, 1885	SEPT. 2, 1964	
402	SARAH E. (CALHOUN) PEPPLE	SEPT. 18, 1884	MAY 30, 1962	
403	PAULINE (PEPPLE) LANGHAM	SEPT. 16, 1925	MAR. 9, 1950	
404	ROBERT N. LANGHAM SGT US ARMY WORLD WAR II	SEPT. 29, 1925	AUG. 6, 1988	ROBERT WAS CREMATED. HIS REMAINS BURIED IN PAULINE'S GRAVE.
405	SAMUEL THEODORE PEPPLE SON OF C. H. & S. E. PEPPLE	SEPT. 8, 1914	AUG. 18, 1924	
406	BARTON A. CALHOUN	AUG. 29, 1866	JULY 3, 1937	DEATH CERTIFICATE LISTS DATE OF BIRTH AS SEPT. 29
407	MINNIE R. (BARKMAN) CALHOUN	AUG. 6, 1871	JULY 29, 1952	
408	MABEL (CALHOUN) BRIDGES	MAY 4, 1904	MAR. 6, 1945	
409	WARREN CALHOUN 30TH INF. A. E. F. WORLD WAR I	JULY 4, 1893	JAN. 23, 1919	
410	RAYMOND C. CRAWFORD	DEC. 22, 1898	DEC. 19, 1961	
411	M. ORA (BUSSARD) CRAWFORD	JULY 10, 1905	FEB. 25, 1967	
412	HOMER L. CRAWFORD US ARMY KOREA	SEPT. 25, 1930	JULY 18, 1975	
413	OLIVE M. (BUSSARD) MELLOTT	MAR. 2, 1889	APR. 19, 1978	DOUBLE STONE
414	RUSSELL M. MELLOTT	APR. 11, 1882	NOV. 24, 1967	
415	ZELMA RUTH MELLOTT	OCT. 27, 1925	FEB. 23, 2008	
416	ANNA B. (WEICHT) BUSSARD	MAR. 6, 1901	NOV. 30, 1971	DOUBLE STONE
417	RAYMOND E. BUSSARD	OCT. 25, 1898	SEPT. 6, 1966	

NUMBER	NAMES/INSCRIPTIONS	BIRTH DATE	DEATH DATE	MISC. INFO.
418	DENNIS DUANE BUSSARD SON OF RAYMOND & ANNA BUSSARD	APR. 24, 1934	NOV. 13, 1939	
419	GEORGE DELMAR BUSSARD	JULY 26, 1937	AUG. 25, 1937	DOUBLE STONE SONS OF RAYMOND AND ANNA BUSSARD
420	CARL DEWEY BUSSARD	MAY 18, 1928	MAY 18, 1928	
421	R. ELLIS CALHOUN	FEB. 6, 1914	APR. 14, 1997	DOUBLE STONE
422	HELEN E. (ZIMMERMAN) CALHOUN	DEC. 1, 1911	DEC. 30, 2002	
423	VERA REBECCA BUSSARD	FEB. 26, 1923	MAR. 26, 1923	DOUBLE STONE CHILDREN OF LESTER & MARY BUSSARD
424	CARROLL LEE BUSSARD	APR. 29, 1928	APR. 29, 1928	
425	LESTER V. BUSSARD	FEB. 7, 1901	JUNE 18, 1973	DOUBLE STONE
426	MARY E. (WEICHT) BUSSARD	SEPT. 28, 1895	JUNE 4, 1967	
427	GLENN L. BUSSARD	APR. 5, 1935	AUG. 5, 1986	
428	MILLARD D. CLARK	JAN. 1, 1846	APR. 26, 1918	
429	ALBERT MCDANIEL	AUG. 22, 1874	JAN. 30, 1942	
430	EMMA J. (CONNER) RITCHEY	APR. 26, 1865	SEPT. 16, 1958	DOUBLE STONE
431	WILLIAM R. RITCHEY	MAY 2, 1854	MAY 6, 1935	
432	MILFORD CALHOUN	NOV. 27, 1891	SEPT. 18, 1968	DOUBLE STONE
433	ELSIE I. (STREIGHT) CALHOUN	FEB. 10, 1894	FEB. 15, 1983	
434	JOHN E. MORRIS	FEB. 13, 1893	FEB. 12, 1972	DOUBLE STONE
435	RUTH A. (WEICHT) MORRIS	MAY 3, 1897	JULY 3, 1967	
436	JACOB R. GORDON	MAR. 12, 1891	AUG. 16, 1967	DOUBLE STONE
437	AMANDA E. (PRICE) GORDON	AUG. 29, 1898	MAR. 1, 1960	
438	ROY JOHN GORDON	APR. 9, 1923	NOV. 2, 1923	
439	CARL H. CLARK	FEB. 20, 1929	SEPT. 6, 1944	
440	JENNIE (BARTON) CLARK	MAR. 28, 1887	MAR. 22, 1974	DOUBLE STONE
441	ANDREW CLARK	MAR. 25, 1883	APR. 22, 1935	
442	EMILY E. CLARK	JAN. 10, 1923	DEC. 9, 1923	
443	JANET P. CLARK	1921	1925	TRIPLE STONE
444	JACOB B. CLARK	APR. 2, 1886	FEB. 11, 1970	
445	MINNIE A. (VEATCH) CLARK	DEC. 19, 1891	OCT. 17, 1968	
446	CLYDE V. CLARK US NAVY WORLD WAR II	APR. 28, 1918	APR. 3, 1979	
447	M. MARIAN (THOMPSON) CLARK	NOV. 17, 1923		DOUBLE STONE MARIAN REMARRIED AND IS NOT BURIED IN THIS PLOT. INFO FROM HER DAUGHTER.

NUMBER	NAMES/INSCRIPTIONS	BIRTH DATE	DEATH DATE	MISC. INFO.
448	RONALD GERALD CLARK US NAVY VIETNAM	SEPT. 13, 1943	JUNE 15, 2003	HIS REMAINS ARE BURIED ON MARIAN'S PLOT.
449	MARION F. CALHOUN	DEC. 30, 1907	MAY 17, 1968	DOUBLE STONE
450	KATHERINE E. (PRICE) CALHOUN	AUG. 23, 1916	MAR. 27, 2006	
451	LORENZO RITCHEY	JAN. 14, 1888	MAY 31, 1966	DOUBLE STONE
452	NELLIE (STAYER) RITCHEY	JAN. 12, 1896	NOV. 18, 1982	
453	WILLIAM D. RITCHEY	DEC. 1, 1919	MAY 7, 1931	DEATH CERTIFICATE STATE BIRTH AS 1918 AND DEATH 1933
454	RUTH E. RITCHEY	1928	1928	
455	MARSHALL K. "BUD" RITCHEY	MAY 20, 1915	APR. 24, 2002	DOUBLE STONE
456	EDNA MAE (SNYDER) RITCHEY	FEB. 12, 1914	APR. 17, 2007	
457	PATRICIA J. IMLER DAU. OF ALFRED & ELDA IMLER	JUNE 22, 1935	JUNE 23, 1935	
458	LINDA GAIL TICE DAU. OF DR. & MRS. HAROLD A. TICE	MAY 12, 1957	JULY 22, 1968	
459	RANDOLPH MELLOTT	NOV. 21, 1904	JULY 9, 1914	
460	BETTY J. MELLOTT	APR. 27, 1932	APR. 27, 1932	
461	SOLOMON F. CALHOUN	DEC. 10, 1896	APR. 29, 1979	
462	V. ELDA (HART) CALHOUN	APR. 19, 1898	NOV. 5, 1969	
463	FRANKLIN J. CALHOUN	DEC. 29, 1863	DEC. 13, 1927	DOUBLE STONE
464	PERMILLA J. (WILKINS) CALHOUN	APR. 19, 1868	MAY 21, 1943	DEATH CERTIFICATE LISTS PERMILLA'S DATE OF BIRTH AS JUNE 13, 1867
465	ORVILLE E. CALHOUN	FEB. 19, 1909	SEPT. 18, 1929	DOUBLE STONE
466	JOSEPHINE L. CALHOUN	NOV. 23, 1902	NOV. 18, 1951	
467	VESTA E. (ROBINETTE) GORDON	MAY 11, 1905	NOV. 24, 1967	DOUBLE STONE
468	WALTER E. GORDON	OCT. 15, 1897	FEB. 1, 1979	
469	CAROL J. GORDON	NOV. 14, 1935	NOV. 20, 1935	TRIPLE STONE
470	KATHRYN GORDON		MAR. 27, 1927	
471	RICHARD V. GORDON		OCT. 4, 1925	
472	JACOB C. CALHOUN AGED 27 YEARS, 3 MONTHS AND 25 DAYS	DEC. 18, 1891	APR. 13, 1919	

NUMBER	NAMES/INSCRIPTIONS	BIRTH DATE	DEATH DATE	MISC. INFO.
473	MINNIE E. (BUSSARD) CALHOUN MELLOTT AGED 63 YEARS, 4 MONTHS AND 11 DAYS	FEB. 2, 1893	JUNE 13, 1956	MINNIE WAS FIRST MARRIED TO JACOB C. CALHOUN.
474	GEORGE K. HART	JAN. 19, 1914	OCT. 2, 1975	DOUBLE STONE
475	MAYE C. (CALHOUN) HART	SEPT. 16, 1915	JULY 20, 1988	
476	HARRY FRANKLIN HOCKENBERY	DEC. 28, 1888	NOV. 30, 1973	THERE ARE FIVE (5) PEOPLE LISTED ON THIS STONE.
477	FLOSSIE M. (MELLOTT) HOCKENBERY WIFE OF HARRY F. HOCKENBERY	OCT. 8, 1892	SEPT. 6, 1964	
478	EUGENE DONIE HOCKENBERY	JULY 30, 1934	OCT. 19, 1938	
479	LAWRENCE H. HOCKENBERY	MAR. 8, 1918	FEB. 5, 1929	
480	ROBERT W. HOCKENBERY	JAN. 27, 1915	MAY 19, 1915	
481	VELMA (CALHOUN) AUGUST	SEPT. 30, 1908	MAR. 14, 2000	DOUBLE STONE
482	JAMES W. AUGUST	MAY 8, 1909	DEC. 13, 1976	
483	JAMES W. WILKINS	MAR. 2, 1904	FEB. 26, 1960	DOUBLE STONE
484	OPAL P. (SHIVELY) WILKINS	FEB. 11, 1908	APR. 23, 1939	
485	SIMON W. CALHOUN	FEB. 16, 1895	APR. 2, 1983	TRIPLE STONE
486	MAUDE E. (CLARK) CALHOUN	OCT. 30, 1904	MAY 6, 1985	
487	ROGER LEE CALHOUN		APR. 3, 1944	
488	ALLEN E. CALHOUN	1932		DOUBLE STONE
489	JOANNE L. (TRUAX) CALHOUN	1938		
490	KEVIN L. CALHOUN	AUG. 9, 1962	AUG. 16, 2005	
491	AARON C. SOLLENBERGER	APR. 7, 1887	AUG. 16, 1938	DOUBLE STONE
492	NORA (WILLIAMS) SOLLENBERGER WIFE OF AARON C. SOLLENBERGER	FEB. 25, 1892	FEB. 24, 1974	
493	VICTORIA M. SOLLENBERGER	FEB. 7, 1918	APR. 22, 1929	
494	ORVILLE B. WILLIAMS	FEB. 10, 1890	JUNE 30, 1971	
495	NELLIE B. (BENNETT) WILLIAMS	JUNE 10, 1889	NOV. 23, 1988	
496	ZONA GALE WILLIAMS	JAN. 7, 1917	NOV. 27, 1939	
497	VAUGHN WILLIAMS	JAN. 1, 1900	FEB. 6, 1987	DOUBLE STONE
498	MAGGIE E. (MILLER) WILLIAMS	NOV. 24, 1903	JULY 12, 1986	
499	ALBERT WILLIAMS MCDANIEL	MAR. 11, 1874	DEC. 24, 1947	

NUMBER	NAMES/INSCRIPTIONS	BIRTH DATE	DEATH DATE	MISC. INFO.
500	ORA FLOY (SNYDER) MCDANIEL	AUG. 3, 1876	FEB. 22, 1964	
501	GLENN SNYDER MCDANIEL	NOV. 10, 1904	AUG. 4, 1954	
502	WILHEMIMA (LILLER) MCDANIEL	OCT. 3, 1908	APR. 5, 1946	
503	CHARLES EDWARD MCDANIEL	SEPT. 27, 1877	JULY 30, 1962	
504	ELIZABETH M. (BOOR) MCDANIEL	JUNE 8, 1878	DEC. 28, 1945	
505	HAROLD W. MCDANIEL	APR. 26, 1901	APR. 6, 1973	
506	GLENN E. MELLOTT	JUNE 27, 1911	SEPT. 19, 1995	DOUBLE STONE
507	MARY A. (BARTON) MELLOTT	AUG. 14, 1916	OCT. 17, 2010	
508	SHIRLEY ANN MELLOTT	OCT. 16, 1942	OCT. 18, 1942	
509	CLARENCE F. BEEGLE	OCT. 29, 1913	JAN. 5, 2011	DOUBLE STONE
510	MILDRED M. (BUSSARD) BEEGLE	APR. 29, 1921	MAR. 25, 2005	
511	LOIS JANE (BEEGLE) CLARK	MAY 28, 1944	AUG. 31, 1988	
512	JEANNE A. BEEGLE	FEB. 27, 1938	MAY 22, 1975	
513	CLARENCE F. BEEGLE, JR.	OCT. 27, 1940	NOV. 13, 1940	
514	WILLIAM B. CALHOUN PVT. MEDICAL DEPT US ARMY WORLD WAR I	MAY 29, 1895	NOV. 18, 1940	
515	ETHEL M. (RICHARDS) CALHOUN	APR. 17, 1898	OCT. 7, 1966	
516	STANLEY J. POTTS PFC US ARMY WORLD WAR II	APR. 28, 1919	OCT. 29, 1990	
517	ELSIE E. (PEPPLE) POTTS	AUG. 5, 1921	APR. 2, 2008	
518	GEORGE C. PEPPLE US NAVY WORLD WAR II	AUG. 25, 1912	APR. 6, 1971	DOUBLE STONE
519	PATRICIA A. (ANDERSON) PEPPLE	1928		
520	GLENN E. PRICE	AUG. 2, 1921	JUNE 1, 2005	
521	ROBERT C. PEPPLE	MAR. 8, 1916	JUNE 13, 1960	DOUBLE STONE PEARLE'S 2ND MARRIAGE WAS TO R. ROLLASON
522	PEARLE B. (BEVINS) PEPPLE	JUNE 25, 1919	SEPT. 5, 1999	
523	WALTER FLOYD MCDANIEL	JULY 8, 1901	JAN. 21, 1973	
524	RUTH (O'BRIEN) MCDANIEL	FEB. 3, 1899	JAN. 25, 1986	
525	WHITNEY MCDANIEL	SEPT. 9, 1955	JAN. 2, 1959	
526	MARY MELINDA TRACY FLOSS MCDANIEL	DEC. 25, 1929	FEB. 5, 2008	

NUMBER	NAMES/INSCRIPTIONS	BIRTH DATE	DEATH DATE	MISC. INFO.
527	ALBERT WILSON MCDANIEL COLONEL US REGULAR ARMY KOREA	APR. 3, 1928	APR. 14, 1985	
528	PAUL WILLIAM MCDANIEL US NAVY WORLD WAR II KOREA	JAN. 31, 1914	DEC. 4, 2005	
529	MILLICENT (DWYER) MCDANIEL	MAR. 25, 1917	APR. 21, 1994	
530	TONY S. WELSH	APR. 8, 1903	JAN. 9, 1997	DOUBLE STONE
531	HAZEL V. (MILLER) WELSH	JULY 4, 1902	JAN. 10, 1985	
532	JAMES H. HERSHBERGER	JAN. 14, 1889	JAN. 1, 1966	DOUBLE STONE
533	MARY K. (KEGG) HERSHBERGER	SEPT. 4, 1892	FEB. 14, 1973	
534	REBECCA H. (HERSHBERGER) O'NEAL	JUNE 4, 1922	SEPT. 27, 2014	DOUBLE STONE
535	LEROY O'NEAL US ARMY WORLD WAR II	JULY 21, 1919	APR. 2, 2012	
536	BERNARD P. CALHOUN, SR. T SGT US ARMY AIR CORPS WORLD WAR II	APR. 16, 1923	AUG. 6, 1989	
537	VANCE G. (GORDON) CALHOUN	SEPT. 18, 1928	DEC. 4, 2011	
538	BERNARD P. CALHOUN, JR.	JAN. 31, 1948	JULY 9, 1967	
539	RALPH H. STUCKEY UA ARMY WORLD WAR II KOREA	MAY 17, 1925	APR. 5, 1987	DOUBLE STONE
540	GLADYS G. (GORDON) STUCKEY	1931		
541	PAUL M. CALHOUN	JAN. 3, 1919	FEB. 11, 2017	
542	EVELYN A. (ANDREWS) CALHOUN	MAY 31, 1917	FEB. 3, 2002	DOUBLE STONE
543	JAMES B. PEPPLE US AIR FORCE	OCT. 17, 1966	AUG. 18, 2001	
544	GROVER CLEVELAND ADAMS SGT US ARMY AIR CORPS 1942 – 1946 WORLD WAR II	JULY 4, 1920	JUNE 1, 1995	DOUBLE STONE MARRIED APRIL 17, 1942
545	OLIVE N. (CALHOUN) ADAMS	NOV. 27, 1922	AUG. 11, 1993	

NUMBER	NAMES/INSCRIPTIONS	BIRTH DATE	DEATH DATE	MISC. INFO.
546	RANDOLPH B. CALHOUN	OCT. 25, 1924	JAN. 8, 1997	DOUBLE STONE
547	ALMA (SPADE) CALHOUN	MAY 17, 1928		
548	DONALD L. PEPPLE PFC US MARINE CORPS	JUNE 30, 1937	DEC. 24, 2011	
549	JOHN E. CHALFANT, JR. F1 US NAVY WORLD WAR II	FEB. 6, 1908	MAY 25, 1977	DOUBLE STONE
550	BERTHA M. (MITCHEM) CHALFANT	DEC. 12, 1914	JULY 15, 1994	
551	MARY C. (CHALFANT) BEEGLE	OCT. 21, 1909	APR. 12, 1988	
552	THEODORE F. JAY US ARMY VIETNAM	APR. 28, 1946	FEB. 15, 2016	
553	WOODROW W. VAUGHN	JAN. 30, 1918	SEPT. 9, 1995	DOUBLE STONE
554	LORRAINE G. (HOCKENBERRY) VAUGHN	AUG. 4, 1925	JUNE 23, 2017	
555	WALTER "HANK" ROBINETTE	JUNE 28, 1934		DOUBLE STONE
556	DOROTHY P. (BAUGHMAN) ROBINETTE	AUG. 7, 1937	NOV. 16, 1992	
557	MERYL C. TEWELL	SEPT. 26, 1911	MAY 28, 1995	DOUBLE STONE
558	CARRIE B. (LEADER) TEWELL	OCT. 2, 1907	NOV. 30, 1989	
559	NANCY G. (SPONSLER) PEPPLE	JAN. 25, 1940		DOUBLE STONE
560	RONALD L. PEPPLE US ARMY	JUNE 17, 1936	SEPT. 2, 2009	
561	ARLENE G. (GORDON) HOLLINGSHEAD	MAR. 21, 1930	SEPT. 2, 1980	
562	ROBERT H. HOLLINGSHEAD SN US NAVY KOREA	AUG. 6, 1929	MAY 24, 1993	
563	DELMAR P. LEADER	AUG. 1, 1935		DOUBLE STONE
564	F. JOANN (ROBINETTE) LEADER	APR. 20, 1942		
565	KAREN ELAINE LEADER DAU. OF D. P. & J. E. LEADER	MAR. 16, 1969	MAR. 16, 1969	
566	PAULA JO LEADER DAU. OF D. P. & J. E. LEADER	JULY 14, 1968	JULY 14, 1968	
567	JOHN W. LEADER	JAN. 27, 1926	APR. 11, 2008	DOUBLE STONE
568	MILDRED E. (SLATES) LEADER	MAR. 30, 1924	JUNE 15, 1978	

NUMBER	NAMES/INSCRIPTIONS	BIRTH DATE	DEATH DATE	MISC. INFO.
569	DONNA M. (BEEGLE) HOCKENBERRY	AUG. 4, 1945		DOUBLE STONE
570	DUANE A. HOCKENBERRY	MAY 10, 1937		
571	DOUGLAS D. HOCKENBERRY	MAY 23, 1968	SEPT. 27, 2015	
572	PAUL E. CLARK	NOV. 5, 1909	DEC. 21, 1977	
573	LYDA C. (SHAFFER) CLARK	FEB. 22, 1910	JAN. 6, 2005	
574	INFANT CLARK SON OF HARRY & JOYCE CLARK		OCT. 18, 1962	
575	WILLIAM LEADER, SR. TEC 5 US ARMY WORLD WAR II	JAN. 30, 1926	JULY 5, 1986	DOUBLE STONE
576	PATRICIA A. (PADGETT) LEADER	AUG. 20, 1941		
577	MICHAEL A. PARKER PFC US ARMY	JULY 8, 1958	FEB. 6, 1994	
578	HAROLD WILSON CALHOUN	MAY 15, 1916	DEC. 29, 1996	DOUBLE STONE
579	DOROTHY IRENE (ZIMMERMAN) CALHOUN	MAR. 22, 1918	FEB. 22, 1989	
580	HUBERT V. CLARK SGT 343RD INF. CO. I. 86TH INF. DIV. EUROPEAN THEATER BLACK HAWKS WORLD WAR II	AUG. 14, 1923	MAY 5, 2000	DOUBLE STONE
581	BETTY J. (WELSH) CLARK	JULY 19, 1924		
582	THEODORE S. CLARK	JUNE 18, 1907	MAR. 9, 1971	DOUBLE STONE
583	L. MAY (SHAFFER) CLARK	MAY 10, 1905	NOV. 29, 2005	
584	RAY EVERETT CLARK US ARMY KOREA	MAY 11, 1931	JUNE 12, 2011	DOUBLE STONE
585	MARGARET JO ANN CLARK	OCT. 22, 1929		
586	ELWOOD S. HOLLIDAY PVT 84TH F. A. BN US ARMY WORLD WAR II	NOV. 30, 1921	OCT. 1961	
587	GERALDINE M. (SALYARDS) HOLLIDAY	NOV. 21, 1921	APR. 8, 1977	DENESE G. DEETERS WAS CREMATED AND BURIED ON THIS GRAVE. SEE #713.

NUMBER	NAMES/INSCRIPTIONS	BIRTH DATE	DEATH DATE	MISC. INFO.
588	ELWOOD CLAYTON HOLLIDAY	DEC. 28, 1941	JAN. 6, 1991	NO STONE. HIS REMAINS WERE PLACED AT THE FOOT OF HIS MOTHER'S GRAVE. (FROM CEMETERY RECORDS)
589	RANDOLPH B. CLARK	MAY 3, 1918	NOV. 26, 2001	
590	BETTY (GRIMES) CLARK	SEPT. 27, 1918	JAN. 16, 2011	
591	CLINTON CLARK US COAST GUARD VIETNAM	MAY 25, 1941	JAN. 29, 2016	
592	ROBERT K. SMITH	FEB. 8, 1929	JAN. 27, 1993	
593	ROBERT JAMES SMITH	JULY 13, 1951	APR. 14, 2008	
594	ROSS V. CALHOUN CPL US ARMY WORLD WAR II	MAY 11, 1920	FEB. 14, 1992	DOUBLE STONE
595	BETTY L. (CLARK) CALHOUN	JUNE 2, 1929		
596	WALTER H. LEADER	DEC. 21, 1909	MAR. 15, 1989	
597	ROSA I. (COLLEDGE) LEADER	FEB. 22, 1908	MAR. 28, 2001	
598	ROY A. GRIMES, JR.	MAY 14, 1923	MAR. 20, 1994	DOUBLE STONE
599	NANCY (O'NEAL) GRIMES			
600	VERA I. CALHOUN	JULY 17, 1926		
601	EDWARD B. CALHOUN US NAVY WORLD WAR II US AIR FORCE KOREA	JAN. 27, 1925		
602	J. FRANK HERSHBERGER	MAY 14, 1892	DEC. 17, 1978	DOUBLE STONE
603	LULA W. (WILLIAMS) HERSHBERGER	MAY 20, 1890	DEC. 16, 1975	
604	GRACE E. (HERSHBERGER) FRITZ	DEC. 2, 1916	NOV. 14, 1981	
605	RUSSEL E. FRITZ	NOV. 29, 1912	NOV. 13, 2007	
606	JOHN LEADER	MAR. 21, 1912	OCT. 15, 1994	DOUBLE STONE
607	MARGARET J. (BROWN) LEADER	JULY 2, 1915	JUNE 4, 2000	
608	G. GARY LEADER	APR. 1, 1942		
609	RAYMOND J. RITCHEY US ARMY AIR FORCE WORLD WAR II	SEPT. 15, 1926	APR. 8, 2009	TRIPLE STONE
610	WESLEY M. RITCHEY	JUNE 24, 1954	MAR. 23, 2002	
611	DORRIS J. (GORDON) RITCHEY	APR. 1927		

NUMBER	NAMES/INSCRIPTIONS	BIRTH DATE	DEATH DATE	MISC. INFO.
612	RONALD C. GORDON US ARMY VIETNAM	MAR. 18, 1933	JUNE 22, 2002	DOUBLE STONE
613	CAROL A. (POINTER) GORDON	1940		
614	DR. NORVIL T. POINTER LT US NAVY WORLD WAR II	MAY 21, 1910	FEB. 18, 1975	DOUBLE STONE
615	CATHERINE M. (ROBERTSON) POINTER	NOV. 27, 1913	FEB. 16, 1977	
616	ANDREW PRONCHAK	DEC. 11, 1893	SEPT. 27, 1985	
617	MARY (PARNICKI) PRONCHAK	AUG. 4, 1899	OCT. 23, 1981	DOUBLE STONE
618	GEORGE D. THOMAS MAJOR US ARMY WORLD WAR II	NOV. 8, 1917	JUNE 8, 2001	DOUBLE STONE MARRIED JUNE 17, 1945
619	CATHARIN (PRONCHAK) THOMAS	FEB. 15, 1921	JAN. 23, 2003	
620	SARA JANE (GORDON) PLUMMER	DEC. 8, 1937		
621	HAROLD WAYNE PLUMMER	JULY 13, 1935		
622	CLARENCE M. COULTER US NAVY WORLD WAR II	JULY 10, 1925	JULY 31, 1968	
623	JOHN FRANKLIN PRICE	JUNE 2, 1941		
624	IVA JEAN (SNYDER) PRICE	MAR. 30, 1941		DOUBLE STONE
625	EUGENE JAY	FEB. 21, 1932		
626	VIRGINIA (GILPIN) JAY	DEC. 19, 1934	MAY 4, 2016	DOUBLE STONE
627	WILLIAM G. FELTON TEC 4 US ARMY WORLD WAR II	JULY 19, 1925	OCT. 10, 1989	
628	G. ARLENE (JAY) FELTON	MAY 13, 1926		
629	GERALD L. BUSSARD	APR. 23, 1945	SEPT. 5, 1971	
630	E. RALPH O'NEAL	JAN. 3, 1904	OCT. 6, 1986	
631	EDNA G. (CALHOUN) O'NEAL	APR. 15, 1910	JUNE 9, 2000	DOUBLE STONE
632	CHESTER L. AULT PFC CO M 351ST INF. PH WORLD WAR II	AUG. 21, 1923	SEPT. 25, 1972	DOUBLE STONE
633	BETTY L. (STEACH) AULT	JUNE 6, 1930		
634	ADA (BUSSARD) ROHRER AGED 53 YEARS AND 4 MONTHS		NOV. 1, 1937	
635	HOWARD B. ROHRER	SEPT. 22, 1877	FEB. 26, 1950	
636	HOWARD S. ROHRER US ARMY WORLD WAR II	NOV. 1, 1902	FEB. 7, 1965	

NUMBER	NAMES/INSCRIPTIONS	BIRTH DATE	DEATH DATE	MISC. INFO.
637	THEODORE (TED) SNYDER	1920	1990	DOUBLE STONE
638	MAXINE (HOCKENBERRY) SNYDER	SEPT. 29, 1926	MAR. 28, 2017	
639	LEE E. HOCKENBERY	1929	2004	
640	HARRY F. HOCKENBERRY, JR.	MAR. 26, 1924	JAN. 18, 2003	DOUBLE STONE
641	MABEL R. (DIVELY) HOCKENBERRY	MAY 11, 1924	AUG. 20, 2012	
642	LUCINDA PEARL (CALHOUN) FOREMAN	AUG. 3, 1897	APR. 27, 1986	
643	VERA M. (CALHOUN) WOLFE	APR. 6, 1912	OCT. 3, 1988	
644	JAMES WOLFE, SR. PVT US ARMY WORLD WAR II	DEC. 27, 1916	FEB. 11, 2004	
645	CHRISTOPHER L. WOLFE	1971	1971	MARKER IS MISSING
646	LOUTRICIA ANN ROBERTS	1970	1970	
647	BOWMAN E. KENNEDY, SR.	MAY 1, 1900	JAN. 12, 1966	DOUBLE STONE
648	VIOLA E. (FOOR) KENNEDY	OCT. 10, 1898	SEPT. 13, 1983	
649	ROY M. PEPPLE	APR. 16, 1941	DEC. 30, 2013	DOUBLE STONE
650	NANCY L. (GRIMES) PEPPLE	FEB. 25, 1943		
651	WM. HOLBERT BRIDGES		JAN. 12, 1947	
652	JOHN OSOLING	JULY 31, 1886	DEC. 28, 1959	
653	ADA (CALHOUN) OSOLING	NOV. 12, 1901	APR. 22, 1951	
654	BRUCE KELLER COLEMAN US NAVY WORLD WAR II	MAY 24, 1925	JULY 28, 2000	DOUBLE STONE
655	DOROTHY MAY (BUSSARD) COLEMAN	OCT. 7, 1924	JULY 31, 1968	
656	STANLEY B. GORDON	APR. 18, 1915	MAY 12, 1993	DOUBLE STONE
657	PAULINE M. (DODSON) GORDON	AUG. 15, 1915	MAR. 24, 1988	
658	RAYMON LEE GORDON, SR.	SEPT. 5, 1926		
659	INEZ M. (FOORE) GORDON	NOV. 22, 1929	MAR. 22, 2008	
660	GERTRUDE E. KOWALSKI	1903	1964	
661	MARGARET M. (REESE) SAMIKOS	FEB. 2, 1923	JUNE 22, 1957	DOUBLE STONE
662	CHARLES E. SHIVELY	APR. 20, 1879	DEC. 31, 1946	
663	ANNA BELLE (GARLAND) SHIVELY	APR. 16, 1888	DEC. 20, 1964	

NUMBER	NAMES/INSCRIPTIONS	BIRTH DATE	DEATH DATE	MISC. INFO.
664	WILLIAM MARCUS SHIVELY EM3 US NAVY WORLD WAR II	JAN. 4, 1912	OCT. 13, 1989	
665	JAMES L. FELTON	AUG. 2, 1924	OCT. 30, 1988	
666	MARJORIE R. (HOOVER) FELTON	MAY 9, 1928		
667	AUSTIN H. RITCHEY US ARMY WORLD WAR II	SEPT. 15, 1926	MAY 9, 1979	
668	DOROTHY I. (LYNCH) RITCHEY	1929	1991	
669	ALBERT K. FOOR	SEPT. 4, 1924	FEB. 29, 2008	DOUBLE STONE
670	VESTA C. (BAUGHMAN) FOOR	1925		
671	GORDON W. GRAEFF US ARMY WORLD WAR II	JUNE 2, 1919	APR. 3, 2005	DOUBLE STONE
672	ESTHER I. (IMES) GRAEFF	JULY 28, 1925	MAR. 14, 2014	
673	HARVEY E. GORDON US ARMY WORLD WAR I	FEB. 14, 1892	JAN. 5, 1968	
674	DOLLY V. (YOUNG) GORDON	OCT. 23, 1905	SEPT. 11, 1978	
675	HARRY J. GORDON	AUG. 30, 1930	SEPT. 9, 1998	
676	RHECY C. WIGFIELD US ARMY WORLD WAR II	OCT. 11, 1919	JUNE 30, 1999	DOUBLE STONE
677	BETTY JANE (BUSSARD) WIGFIELD	MAR. 9, 1925	DEC. 11, 2013	
678	DAVID LEADER, JR.	DEC. 31, 1920	DEC. 1, 2013	DOUBLE STONE
679	JEWEL C. (BISHOP) LEADER	JULY 22, 1921	JULY 1, 2008	
680	LAVERNE C. (LEADER) BOLLMAN	OCT. 2, 1948		DOUBLE STONE
681	PHILIP B. BOLLMAN LCPL US MARINE CORPS VIETNAM	MAY 31, 1942	AUG. 26, 2015	
682	CHRISTINE FORDHAM	1988	1988	
683	GEORGE W. PRICE	FEB. 2, 1906	JAN. 29, 1991	DOUBLE STONE
684	VOLNA R. (POTTS) PRICE	DEC. 16, 1908	NOV. 23, 1987	
685	LORENZO N. RITCHEY, JR.	AUG. 30, 1932		DOUBLE STONE
686	VIVIAN M. (IMES) RITCHEY	MAR. 25, 1932	JULY 31, 2015	
687	INFANT BUSSARD SON OF L. V. & M. E. BUSSARD	APR. 29, 1928	APR. 29, 1928	
688	VERA BUSSARD DAU. OF L. V. & M. E. BUSSARD	FEB. 26, 1923	MAR. 23, 1923	

NUMBER	NAMES/INSCRIPTIONS	BIRTH DATE	DEATH DATE	MISC. INFO.
689	MINNIE MAE CALHOUN DAU. OF BART AND MINNIE CALHOUN	MAY 1, 1907	JAN. 29, 2001	
690	LINDA SUE CHALFANT	JULY 6, 1964	APR. 19, 2003	NO STONE
691	JENNIE (HEDGES) CRISSEY SECOND WIFE OF JOHN C. CRISSEY	MAY 18, 1856	OCT. 21, 1909	
692	TINA MARIE (CHILDERS) KALFAS	AUG. 18, 1965	APR. 15, 1997	BURIED UNDER MAIDEN NAME
693	CHRISTINA E. GORDON WIFE OF CHARLES GORDON	JULY 24, 1867	JAN. 31, 1935	
694	SARA LOUISE HANN DAU. OF OLIVER REEP AND F. E. HANN		DEC. 26, 1946	
695	SHELI ANN HOCKENBERRY DAU. OF DUANE AND IRMA HOCKENBERRY			
696	INFANT HOLLIDAY DAU. OF ELWOOD S. AND GERALDINE M. HOLLIDAY	SEPT. 6, 1940	SEPT. 6, 1940	
697	ADA IMLER DAU. OF L. TROUT AND C. M. IMLER	OCT. 24, 1897	APR. 19, 1942	
698	NANCY ANN (COOPER) LUSE DAU. OF ALMA I. COOPER	SEPT. 30, 1942	OCT. 4, 2001	
699	ELIZABETH ELLEN (LEADER) MAUK WIFE OF GEORGE MAUK	MAR. 28, 1880	MAY 12, 1956	
700	MARY (GILBERG) MCGEE AGED 71 YEARS		JULY 13, 1939	BURIED UNDER MAIDEN NAME
701	PATRICIA JOAN MILLER	JUNE 22, 1935	JUNE 22, 1935	
702	JENNIE (CLARK) QUAIL WIFE OF WILLIAM J. QUAIL AGED 79 YEARS		SEPT. 17, 1935	
703	ABRAM RITCHEY AGED 74 YEARS		OCT. 5, 1922	
704	MATILDA (MARTIN) RITCHEY WIFE OF ABRAM RITCHEY	AUG. 27, 1856	MAR. 28, 1937	
705	MILDRED M. (FOOR) SALYARDS	OCT. 13, 1900	NOV. 5, 1955	
706	SAMUEL H. SALYARDS	1900	DEC. 1964	
707	MILDRED BIRTHA SALYARDS	APR. 7, 1918	DEC. 2, 1919	

NUMBER	NAMES/INSCRIPTIONS	BIRTH DATE	DEATH DATE	MISC. INFO.
708	PAUL EUGENE SALYARDS	MAY 1, 1928	MAY 23, 1928	
709	JOHN R. SAMIKOS AGED 12 DAYS		MAY 3, 1935	ACCORDING TO JOHN'S DEATH CERTIFICATE HE WAS A TWIN.
710	OLETA BELLE SHIVELY DAU. OF CHARLES E. AND ANNA BELLE (GARLAND) SHIVELY	DEC. 11, 1925	JUNE 13, 2003	
711	JULIE MARIE WEAVERLING	1971	1971	GRANDDAUGHTER OF CLYDE & MARIAN CLARK
712	WILMA M. GORDON	MAY 23, 1937	MAY 21, 2017	
713	DENESE G. DEETERS		MAR. 9, 2017	THIS WAS A CREMATION. SHE IS BURIED ON THE GRAVE OF GERALDINE M. (SALYARDS) HOLLIDAY. SEE #587.
714	RITA CALHOUN	NOV. 22, 1929	JAN. 14, 2018	

NOTES

NOTES

O'Neal Farm Cemetery

Documented: Early 2017

This cemetery is located on private property. Please ask permission from landowner prior to entering. According to an earlier read of this cemetery that I found at the Bedford County Historical Society that was done in the 1930's, Sarah O'Neal is buried in this cemetery. When I visited this cemetery there were five stones still standing. Sarah's stone is present in the cemetery but is almost unreadable. I was able to compare the dates that I was able to read to the dates from the previous read to confirm this is indeed Sarah's stone.

GPS Coordinates

39.968945, -78.364430

Address

160 West Mattie Road

Everett, PA 15537

Cemetery List

NUMBER	NAMES/INSCRIPTIONS	BIRTH DATE	DEATH DATE	MISC. INFO.
1	ANNA E. O'NEAL AGED 71 YEARS, 10 MONTHS AND 16 DAYS		JAN. 2, 1907	
2	JOHN HARVEY O'NEAL	NOV. 6, 1837	OCT. 3, 1917	
3	CATHERINE O'NEAL WIFE OF JAMES O'NEAL AGED 56 YEARS AND 3 DAYS		MAY 12, 1848	
4	JAMES O'NEAL AGED 77 YEARS, 11 MONTHS AND 23 DAYS		NOV. 4, 1869	
5	SARAH O'NEAL DAU. OF JAMES AND CATHERINE O'NEAL		SEPT. 21, 1871	PLEASE SEE NOTE ON PREVIOUS PAGE.

NOTES

NOTES

Ritchey Farm Cemetery

Documented: Summer of 2017

This cemetery is located on private property. Please ask permission from landowner prior to entering.

GPS Coordinates

40.051932, -78.320157

Address

1115 Ritchey Bridge Road

Everett, PA 15537

Cemetery List

NUMBER	NAMES/INSCRIPTIONS	BIRTH DATE	DEATH DATE	MISC. INFO.
1	ELI CHAMBERLAIN	NOV. 19, 1785	NOV. 12, 1812	STONE IS BROKEN AND IN MANY PIECES
2	ADAM RITCHEY AGED 72 YEARS, 10 MONTHS AND 6 DAYS		NOV. 4, 1830	
3	AUGUSTUS RITCHEY		AUGUST 7, 1827	THIS IS A HAND CARVED STONE.
4	CATHERINE RITCHEY WIFE OF DANIEL RITCHEY			NO OTHER DATES OR INSCRIPTIONS ON THIS STONE.
5	CATHERINE RITCHEY DIED IN HER 74 YEAR		JUNE 15, 1834	
6	DANIEL RITCHEY AGED 66 YEARS, 7 MONTHS AND 21 DAYS		1862	THIS STONE IS DAMAGED AND BROKEN. VERY HARD TO READ.

NUMBER	NAMES/INSCRIPTIONS	BIRTH DATE	DEATH DATE	MISC. INFO.
7	DAVID RITCHEY SON OF DANIEL AND CATHARINE RITCHEY CIVIL WAR CO. J. 208TH REGT. P. V. DIED IN FRONT OF PETERSBURG AGED 29 YEARS, 2 MONTHS AND 4 DAYS		JAN. 21, 1865	
8	JACOB RITCHEY	1798	1865	
9	MARY JANE RITCHEY DAU. OF DANIEL AND CATHERINE RITCHEY AGED 24 YEARS, 8 MONTHS AND 10 DAYS		JUNE 3, 1863	
10	J. BARNDOLLAR ROHM AGED 7 YEARS, 6 MONTHS AND 29 DAYS		DEC. 20, 1858	
11	BARBARA (SWARTZ) SPARKS RITCHEY			SEE PLAQUE TRANSCRIPTION ON FOLLOWING PAGE.
12	HENRY SWARTZ CO. I 194TH REG. PV	NOV. 14, 1847	1873	
13	BROKEN STONE WITH INSCPRIPTION "H. WINTERNIGHT, JR."			
14	J. R. 1834			LARGE STONE WITH ROUNDED TOP

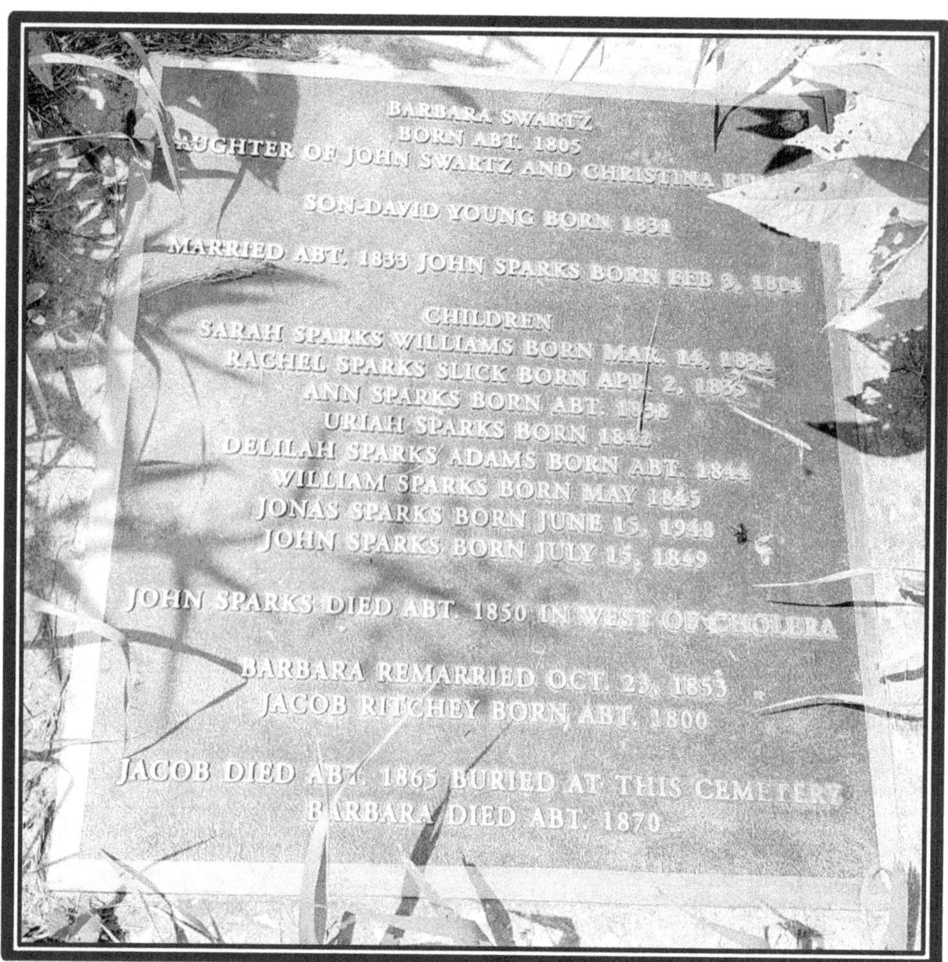

Plaque in Ritchey Cemetery
(transcription below)

Barbara Swartz, Born about 1805, Daughter of John Swartz and Christina Rinard
Son, David Young, Born 1831
Married about 1833, John Sparks, Born Feb. 3, 1804
Children:
Sarah Sparks Williams, Born March 14, 1834
Rachel Sparks Slick, Born April 2, 1835
Ann Sparks, Born about 1838
Uriah Sparks, Born about 1842
Delilah Sparks Adams, Born about 1844
William Sparks, Born about 1845
Jonas Sparks, Born June 15, 1848
John Sparks, Born July 15, 1849
John Sparks died about 1850 in West of Cholera.
Barbara remarried October 23, 1853
Jacob Ritchey, Born about 1800
Jacob died about 1865, buried at this cemetery.
Barbara died about 1870.

NOTES

NOTES

Roller/Disbrow Farm Cemetery

This cemetery is located on private property. Please ask permission from landowner prior to entering. I documented this cemetery during the fall of 2017. Only two stones are currently visible in this cemetery, it is full of groundhog holes and this is probably the reason the other stones are not visible. There were a few attempts to find additional stones in this cemetery but they were unsuccessful.

GPS Coordinates

39.964610, -78.349576

Address

Menchtown Road

Everett, PA 15537

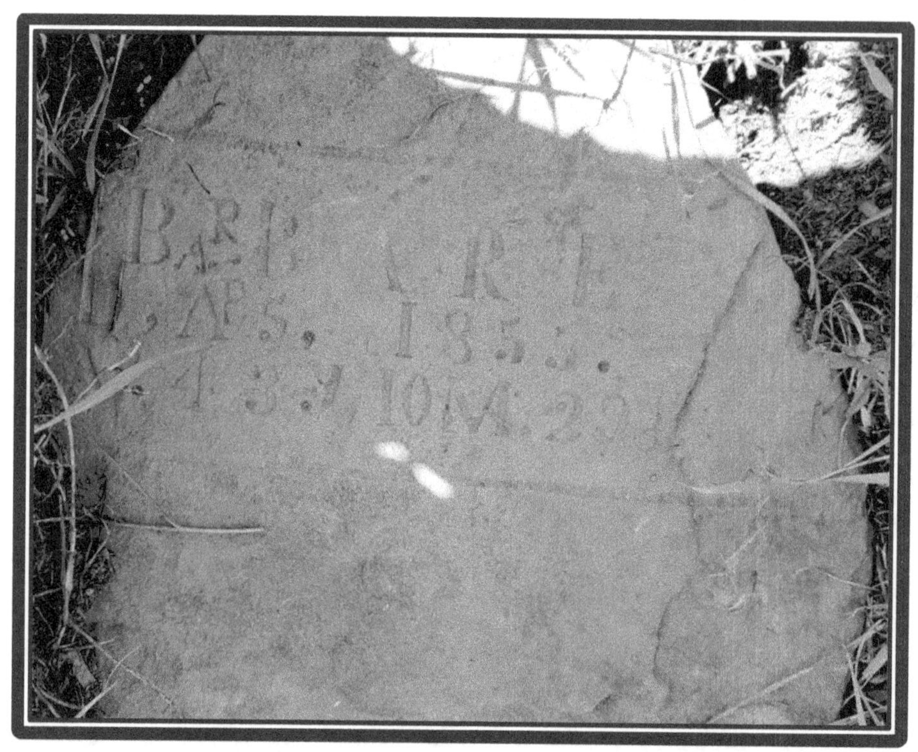
BARBARA R...
D. AP. 5, 185..
A. 3 , 10 M. 29 ...

In
Memory of
CATHERINE,
Wife of
JONATHAN ROLLER
Born Oct. 11, 178.1
Died Nov. 30, 1858,
Aged 74 ys. 1 mo. 15 d.

Cemetery List

NUMBER	NAMES/INSCRIPTIONS	BIRTH DATE	DEATH DATE	MISC. INFO.
1	BARB ARE AGED 43 YEARS, 10 MONTHS AND 29 DAYS		APRIL 5, 1855	THIS STONE IS STILL IN THE CEMETERY.
2	CATHERINE ROLLER WIFE OF JONATHAN ROLLER AGED 74 YEARS, 1 MONTH AND 19 DAYS	OCT. 11, 1784	NOV. 30, 1858	THIS STONE IS STILL IN THIS CEMETERY.
3	JONATHAN ROLLER AGED 71 YEARS AND 27 DAYS	AUG. 28, 1792	SEPT. 25, 1862	THESE STONES ARE NO LONGER IN THE CEMETERY. THIS INFORMATION WAS FROM A READING DONE IN THE 1930'S
4	ANN ELIZABETH ROLLER AGED 70 YEARS, 11 MONTHS AND 7 DAYS	JAN. 26, 1784	JAN. 2, 1855	
5	ELIZABETH DISBROW AGED ABOUT 65 YEARS		OCT. 19, 1871	
6	REBECCA DISBROW WIFE OF JOHN DISBROW AGED 71 YEARS, 9 MONTHS AND 23 DAYS		JULY 9, 1871	
7	JOHN DISBROW AGED 76 YEARS, 4 MONTHS AND 15 DAYS		DEC. 25, 1876	

NOTES

Sparks Cemetery

Documented: Summer of 2017

GPS Coordinates

39.993428, -78.353213

Address

Calhoun Road

Everett, PA 15537

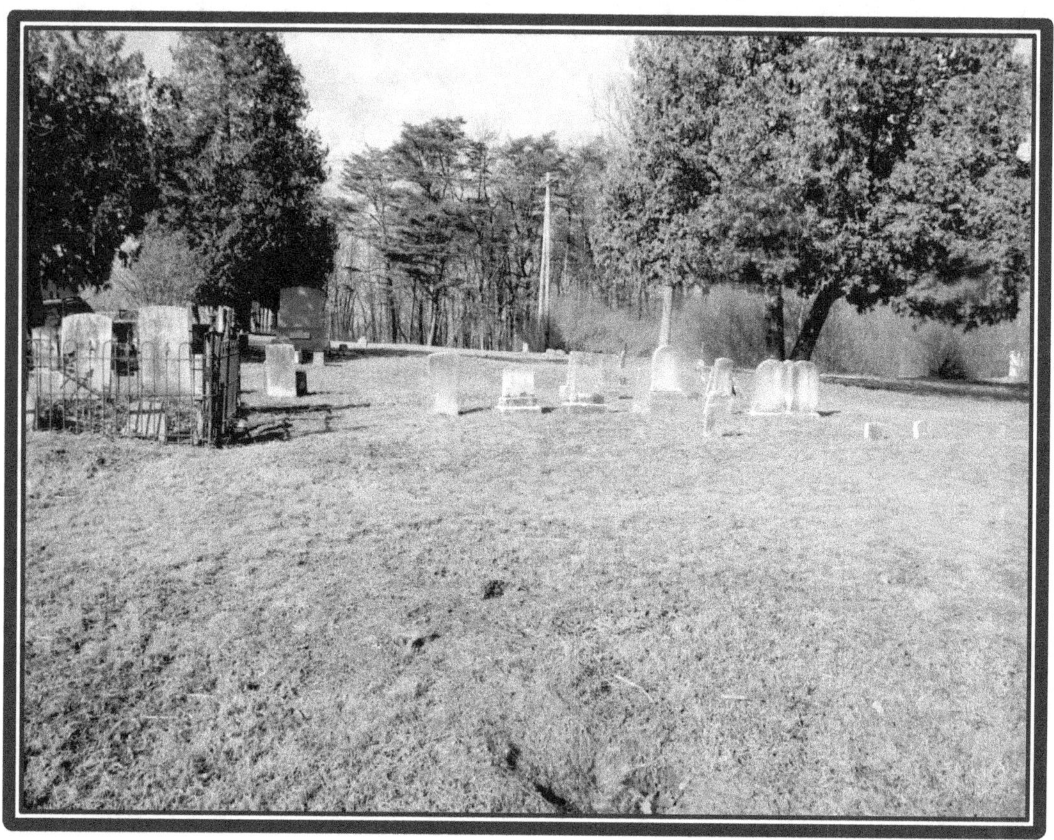

Cemetery List

NUMBER	NAMES/INSCRIPTIONS	BIRTH DATE	DEATH DATE	MISC. INFO.
1	CHARLOTTE S. MILLS WIFE OF JOHN L. MILLS AGED 78 YEARS, 8 MONTHS AND 25 DAYS		DEC. 23, 1893	DOUBLE STONE
2	JOHN L. MILLS AGED 70 YEARS, 7 MONTHS AND 8 DAYS		NOV. 3, 1878	
3	INFANT MILLS DAU. OF L. & E. MILLS	FEB. 8, 1890		
4	JOAN AILEEN SPONSLER DAU. OF A. L. & L. A. SPONSLER	SEPT. 27, 1936	SEPT. 30, 1936	
5	GRACE GRIMES DAU. OF H. & M. E. GRIMES		OCT. 25, 1909	
6	WILLIAM K. PEPPLE AGED 72 YEARS, 2 MONTHS AND 24 DAYS		NOV. 19, 1903	
7	FANNIE HEISTER PEPPLE WIFE OF WILLIAM PEPPLE AGED 81 YEARS, 8 MONTHS AND 20 DAYS		MAR. 8, 1931	
8	ZORA ANN COLLAGE AGED 21 YEARS AND 2 MONTHS		JUNE 7, 1891	
9	SAMUEL TAYLOR PEPPLE SON OF W. & F. PEPPLE AGED 6 MONTHS AND 28 DAYS		MAR. 19, 1881	
10	WILLIAM E. PEPPLE AGED 49 YEARS, 5 MONTHS AND 18 DAYS	JULY 7, 1875	DEC. 25, 1924	
11	JAMES SPARKS AGED 72 YEARS, 10 MONTHS AND 11 DAYS CO. K 203RD P. V.		JAN. 23, 1904	
12	MARGARET SPARKS WIFE OF JAMES SPARKS AGED 43 YEARS AND 11 MONTHS AND 14 DAYS		FEB. 12, 1879	
13	WILLIAM A. SPARKS SON OF J. & M. SPARKS AGED 4 YEARS, 1 MONTH AND 17 DAYS		NOV. 26, 1880	

NUMBER	NAMES/INSCRIPTIONS	BIRTH DATE	DEATH DATE	MISC. INFO.
14	DAVID C. SPARKS AGED 79 YEARS, 8 MONTHS AND 6 DAYS CO. K 208TH REGT. CIVIL WAR	OCT. 24, 1838	JAN. 30, 1917	
15	ABSALOM SPARKS AGED 58 YEARS		JUNE 3, 1862	
16	HENRY SPARKS SON OF A. & M. SPARKS AGED 3 YEARS AND 9 MONTHS		JULY 30, 1838	
17	MAHALAH SPARKS WIFE OF ABSALOM SPARKS		FEB. 29, 1888	
18	JAMES H. SPARKS AGED 76 YEARS, 4 MONTHS AND 11 DAYS CO. K. 208TH AND 133RD REGT'S PA INF.	JUNE 2, 1841	OCT. 13, 1917	DOUBLE STONE
19	ELIZABETH C. SPARKS	DEC. 18, 1840	NO DEATH DATE INSCRIPTION	PENNSYLVANIA DEATH CERTIFICATE #5658 LISTS ELIZABETH'S DEATH DATE AS JAN. 3, 1928
20	JACOB SPARKS DIED NEAR FREDERICKSBURG, VA WHILE A MEMBER OF CO. K, 133RD REGT. PA VOL. AGED 24 YEARS, 9 MONTHS AND 14 DAYS		NOV. 16, 1863	
21	PHILIP W. SPARKS AGED 33 YEARS, 1 MONTH AND 21 DAYS		APRIL 7, 1878	
22	DAVID E. SPARKS SON OF P. W. & R. V. SPARKS AGED 8 YEARS, 7 MONTHS AND 20 DAYS		DEC. 21, 1883	

NUMBER	NAMES/INSCRIPTIONS	BIRTH DATE	DEATH DATE	MISC. INFO.
23	DAVID C. WILLIAMS SON OF JOHN & ANN E. WILLIAMS		APRIL 1_, 1841	
24	INFANT SPARKS SON OF P. W. & R. V. SPARKS		OCT. 21, 1877	
25	SARAH ANN SPARKS WIFE OF DAVID SPARKS AGED 55 YEARS, 1 MONTH AND 27 DAYS		JUNE 12, 1869	DOUBLE STONE
26	DAVID SPARKS AGED 60 YEARS, 1 MONTH AND 2 DAYS		JUNE 13, 1869	
27	INFANT SPARKS SON OF DAVID & SARAH SPARKS		FEB. 25, 1841	DOUBLE STONE
28	ANN ELIZA SPARKS DAU. OF DAVID & SARAH SPARKS AGED 10 DAYS		MAY 6, 1843	
29	DAVID WEEKS SON OF W. L. & C. WEEKS AGED 4 YEARS AND 1 DAY		SEPT. 1, 1836	
30	ELIZABETH WEEKS WIFE OF W. L. WEEKS	APRIL 29, 1811	FEB. 17, 1888	
31	WILSON L. WEEKS	JAN. 10, 1810	NOV. 27, 1885	
32	ANN SPARKS WIFE OF JAMES SPARKS AGED 63 YEARS, 1 MONTH AND 6 DAYS		JAN. 10, 1832	
33	CATHERINE SPARKS WIFE OF DANIEL SPARKS AGED 73 YEARS, 9 MONTHS AND 19 DAYS		MAY 5, 1889	
34	DANIEL SPARKS AGED 70 YEARS, 8 MONTHS AND 20 DAYS		MAY 30, 1877	
35	WILLIAM HENRY SPARKS SON OF S. & S. SPARKS AGED 4 YEARS, 5 MONTHS AND 21 DAYS		APRIL 7, 1817	
36	HENRY H. HIXON	1840	1932	DOUBLE STONE
37	ANNA R. HIXON	1852	1868	
38	MARY SPARKS WIFE OF JAMES SPARKS		JAN. 16, 1851	

NUMBER	NAMES/INSCRIPTIONS	BIRTH DATE	DEATH DATE	MISC. INFO.
39	ELIZABETH FOOR WIFE OF JACOB I. FOOR AGED 77 YEARS, 2 MONTHS AND 26 DAYS		FEB. 25, 1908	
40	FIELD STONE NO INSCRIPTION			
41	FIELD STONE NO INSCRIPTION			
42	FIELD STONE NO INSCRIPTION			
43	ALBERT B. ESHELMAN	AUG. 13, 1856	MAR. 18, 1931	THIS IS AN UNMARKED GRAVE. INFORMATION FROM PENNSYLVANIA DEATH CERTIFICATE #27184
44	REBECCA ESHELMAN	JUNE 25, 1855	SEPT. 2, 1918	THIS IS AN UNMARKED GRAVE. INFORMATION FROM PENNSYLVANIA DEATH CERTIFICATE #98519

NOTES

NOTES

West Providence Bible Baptist Church Cemetery

Documented: Fall of 2017

This cemetery is divided into three sections. Special thanks to Ron McFarland who provided me with information on Section 2 of this cemetery.

GPS Coordinates

40.028158, -78.333158

Address

Bunker Hill Road

Everett, PA 15537

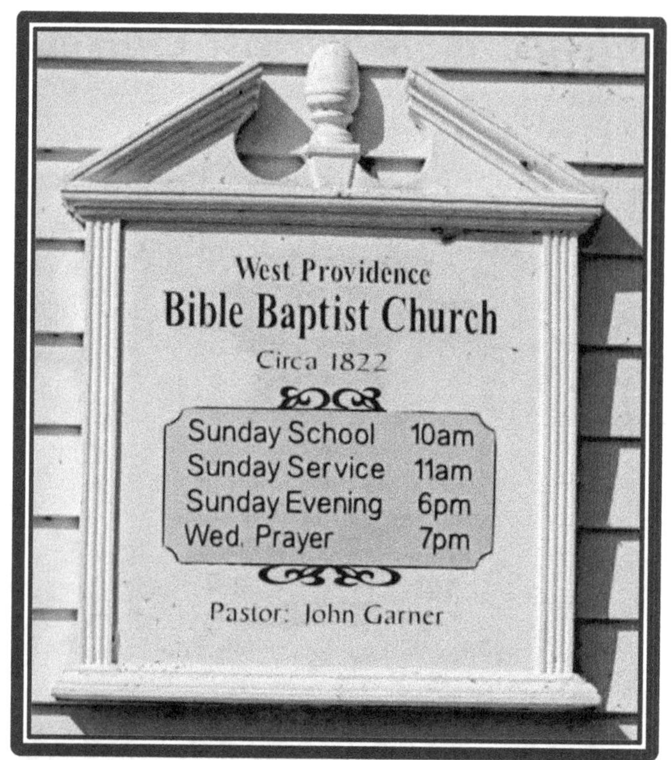

West Providence
Bible Baptist Church
Circa 1822
Sunday School   10am
Sunday Service   11am
Sunday Evening   6pm
Wed. Prayer   7pm
Pastor: John Garner

Cemetery Map

(Section Numbers are referenced in the documentation on the following pages)

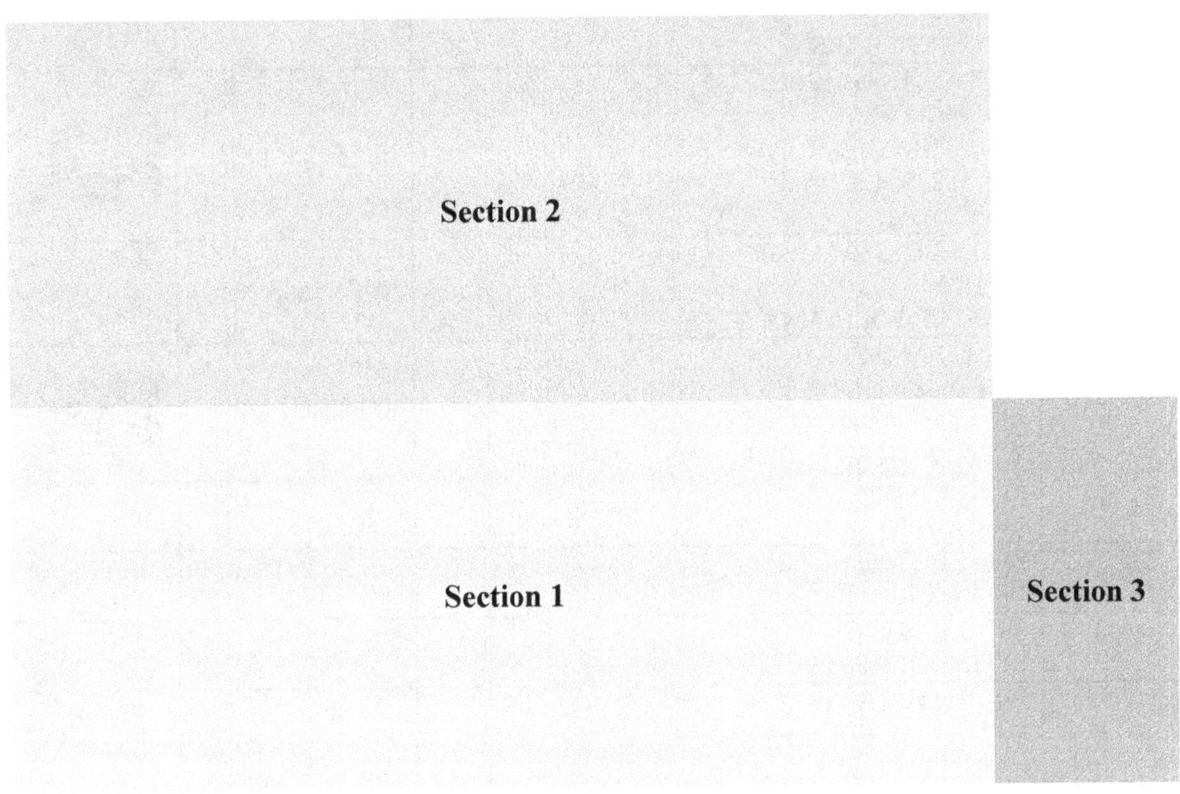

Roadway between church and cemetery

Church

Cemetery List (Section 1)

NUMBER	NAMES/INSCRIPTIONS	BIRTH DATE	DEATH DATE	MISC. INFO.
1	STONE INSCRIBED A. S.			
2	JANE E. GARLICK WIFE OF NICHOLAS GARLICK AGED 68 YEARS		SEPT. 8, 1911	
3	NICHOLAS GARLICK AGED 71 YEARS, 2 MONTHS AND 17 DAYS CO. H 22ND PA CAV. CIVIL WAR		SEPT. 28, 1913	
4	MADELINE SWARTZ LATTA WIFE OF WILLIAM LATTA		MAY 1888	
5	WILLIAM LATTA AGED 68 YEARS, 2 MONTHS AND 27 DAYS CIVIL WAR		SEPT. 8, 1877	
6	FLAT STONE INSCRIBED OUR TWINS			
7	SMALL STONE NO INSCRIPTION			
8	SMALL STONE NO INSCRIPTION			
9	SARAH C. LATTA DAU. OF WILLIAM AND BARBARA LATTA AGED 2 YEARS, 3 MONTHS AND 3 DAYS		DEC. 13, 1862	
10	JANE LATTA			
11	SARAH SPARKS AGED 73 YEARS, 8 MONTHS AND 27 DAYS		SEPT. 13, 1860	
12	ABRAHAM SPARKS AGED 63 YEARS, 10 MONTHS AND 10 DAYS		DEC. 18, 1854	
13	RACHEL SPARKS WIFE OF SOLOMON SPARKS AGED 77 YEARS, 4 MONTHS AND 20 DAYS		FEB. 13, 1842	
14	SOLOMON SPARKS AGED 77 YEARS, 8 MONTHS AND 25 DAYS PVT BOYDS BEDFORD RANGERS REVOLUTIONARY WAR CAPT 2 REGT PENN RIFLEMAN WAR OF 1812	JULY 13, 1760	APRIL 8, 1838	

NUMBER	NAMES/INSCRIPTIONS	BIRTH DATE	DEATH DATE	MISC. INFO.
15	SMALL STONE NO INCRIPTION			
16	SMALL STONE NO INSCRIPTION			
17	DELILAH HUGHES WIFE OF URIAH HUGHES AGED 75 YEARS, 3 MONTHS AND 7 DAYS		NOV. 25, 1875	
18	URIAH HUGHES AGED 70 YEARS, 11 MONTHS AND 1 DAYS		SEPT. 17, 1866	
19	WILLIAM C. HUGHES AGED 80 YEARS, 1 MONTH AND 19 DAYS	NOV. 6, 1834	DEC. 25, 1914	
20	THOMAS A. STOUT	JULY 8, 1890	JAN. 26, 1975	
21	INFANT BLANKLEY DAU. OF U. AND E. BLANKLEY		MAY 16, 1906	
22	DAVID RILEY SON OF J. AND R. A. RILEY AGED 11 MONTHS AND 1 DAY		SEPT. 2, 1838	
23	DAVID SPEAKER AGED ABOUT 70 YEARS		MAR. 25, 1844	DOUBLE STONE
24	MARY SPEAKER WIFE OF DAVID SPEAKER AGED ABOUT 75 YEARS		MAY 10, 1853	
25	ELIZA J. RILEY DAU. OF J. AND R. A. RILEY AGED 12 YEARS, 11 MONTHS AND 15 DAYS		SEPT. 8, 1843	
26	JOHN RILEY AGED 56 YEARS, 4 MONTHS AND 27 DAYS		MAR. 28, 1864	
27	SAMUEL F. ARMSTRONG SON OF J. AND S. ARMSTRONG		JAN. 5, 1878	
28	ADAM GARLICK AGED 66 YEARS, 4 MONTHS AND 6 DAYS CO. K 12TH PA CAV.		JAN. 19, 1901	
29	JAMES M. MCCLURE	1850	1924	
30	JOHN M. MCCLURE	1847	1925	
31	LEVI CRAWFORD SON OF J. AND T. CRAWFORD AGED 29 YEARS AND 5 MONTHS US MARINE CORPS		AUG. 11, 1910	

NUMBER	NAMES/INSCRIPTIONS	BIRTH DATE	DEATH DATE	MISC. INFO.
32	ESTHER CRAWFORD MCFARLAND	1877	1926	
33	JOSEPH CRAWFORD CO. B 15TH WEST VIRGINIA CIVIL WAR	1846	1933	DOUBLE STONE
34	TILITHA CRAWFORD	1845	1930	
35	INFANT DAU. OF ___. AND ___. SMITH		DEC. 23, 1898	STONE WAS PARTIALLY READABLE. THE INITIALS OF THE PARENTS WERE UNCLEAR.
36	MARY GORDON HINISH	JULY 30, 1870	FEB. 20, 1937	
37	HARRY S. GORDON AGED 4 YEARS AND 9 MONTHS		JAN. 2, 1913	
38	ARLIE H. GORDON AGED 22 YEARS AND 7 MONTHS		NOV. 26, 1912	
39	IDA C. MCFARLAND AGED 34 YEARS, 5 MONTHS AND 23 DAYS	MAR. 31, 1876	SEPT. 23, 1910	
40	HENRY V. CLAUSE AGED 82 YEARS, 1 MONTH AND 15 DAYS		OCT. 22, 1890	
41	ANNIE ELIZABETH STECKMAN	APRIL 13, 1872	MAR. 30, 1943	
42	GEORGE E. SHOWALTER AGED 31 YEARS, 4 MONTHS AND 12 DAYS		MAY 11, 1907	
43	ELLASETTEA MCFARLAND WIFE OF D. MCFARLAND AGED 33 YEARS, 8 MONTHS AND 12 DAYS		JUNE 12, 1883	
44	DANIEL MCFARLAND CO. F 8TH PA RESERVES CO. H 12TH PA CAV. AGED 62 YEARS, 11 MONTHS AND 7 DAYS		JULY 16, 1901	
45	ABRAHAM WILSON SON OF P. AND R. WILSON AGED 1 YEAR AND 8 DAYS		MAR. 24, 1872	
46	JOHN RITCHEY	1870	1872	
47	WILLIAM RITCHEY	1872	1872	
48	SAMUEL RITCHEY	1873	1873	
49	ROY RITCHEY	1889	1889	
50	OSCAR RITCHEY	1889	1889	

NUMBER	NAMES/INSCRIPTIONS	BIRTH DATE	DEATH DATE	MISC. INFO.
51	DAVID U. RITCHEY	1873	1942	
52	CORA A. RITCHEY WIFE OF DAVID U. RITCHEY AGED 42 YEARS, 8 MONTHS AND 20 DAYS		OCT. 21, 1915	
53	JOHN HARALD RITCHEY SON OF D. U. AND C. A. RITCHEY AGED 11 MONTHS AND 27 DAYS		SEPT. 3, 1902	
54	HERBERT STANLEY RITCHEY SON OF D. U. AND C. A. RITCHEY AGED 1 YEAR, 4 MONTHS AND 5 DAYS		JULY 22, 1911	
55	L. MAUDE RITCHEY	AUG. 17, 1879	APRIL 5, 1963	
56	SAMUEL GALBREATH AGED 55 YEARS AND 9 DAYS		MAY 26, 1852	
57	DANIEL W. GORDON	MAY 18, 1896	FEB. 8, 1947	
58	SUSAN A. SPARKS	NOV. 2, 1880	JUNE 8, 1952	
59	HARRY A. SPARKS	AUG. 18, 1877	OCT. 11, 1933	
60	BARBARA E. SPARKS RITCHEY WIFE OF EARL S. RITCHEY	1897	1953	
61	EARL S. RITCHEY WORLD WAR I	1897	1961	
62	WILLIAM MORGART	1870	1930	
63	BURKE ARNOLD RITCHEY SON OF EARL AND ELLA RITCHEY AGED 7 MONTHS AND 6 DAYS	JUNE 25, 1923	FEB. 1, 1924	
64	HARRY CLINTON RITCHEY SON OF JAMES AND BLANCHE RITCHEY	JUNE 2, 1922	OCT. 15, 1922	
65	JOHN SPARKS CO. I 194TH PA VOL. CIVIL WAR	JULY 15, 1849	JAN. 23, 1900	
66	REBECCA J. SPARKS WIFE OF JOHN SPARKS AGED 38 YEARS, 11 MONTHS AND 11 DAYS	MAR. 6, 1853	FEB. 24, 1892	
67	HARRY SLEIGHTER SON OF SIMON AND MARY SLEIGHTER		1872	

NUMBER	NAMES/INSCRIPTIONS	BIRTH DATE	DEATH DATE	MISC. INFO.
68	GEORGE SLEIGHTER SON OF SIMON AND MARY SLEIGHTER		1877	
69	IDA SLEIGHTER DAU. OF SIMON AND MARY SLEIGHTER		1879	
70	MINNIE SLEIGHTER DAU. OF SIMON AND MARY SLEIGHTER		1893	
71	JOSEPH SLEIGHTER	1837	1904	DOUBLE
72	SARAH SLEIGHTER	1834	1914	STONE
73	MARY ANN SLEIGHTER WIFE OF JOSEPH SLEIGHTER AGED 35 YEARS 11 MONTHS AND 21 DAYS		OCT. 2, 1865	
74	STONE BASE NO INSCRIPTION			
75	STONE BASE NO INSCRIPTION			
76	STONE BASE NO INSCRIPTION			
77	STONE BASE NO INSCRIPTION			
78	SAMUEL SHAFER CO. K. 133RD REGT P. V. I.	JAN. 1, 1833	FEB. 6, 1908	
79	HARRIET SHAFER WIFE OF SAMUEL SHAFER	JUNE 12, 1844	JUNE 20, 1917	
80	HARRY S. SHAFER SON OF S. AND H. A. SHAFER AGED 19 YEARS, 4 MONTHS AND 8 DAYS		DEC. 18, 1887	
81	FRANKIE A. SHAFER SON OF S. AND H. A. SHAFER AGED 7 YEARS, 2 MONTHS AND 18 DAYS		OCT. 29, 1875	
82	J. HOWARD SHAFER SON OF S. AND H. A. SHAFER AGED 13 YEARS, 3 MONTHS AND 17 DAYS		FEB. 6, 1894	
83	ELLA M. SIMMONS		OCT. 12, 1871	
84	WILLIE SIMMONS		FEB. 7, 1882	
85	ROSA SIMMONS		APRIL 23, 1873	
86	CHRISTOPHER OSBORN AGED 83 YEARS, 1 MONTH AND 13 DAYS		SEPT. 26, 1872	

NUMBER	NAMES/INSCRIPTIONS	BIRTH DATE	DEATH DATE	MISC. INFO.
87	MARY OSBORN AGED 81 YEARS, 9 MONTHS AND 27 DAYS		MAY 19, 1875	
88	GEORGE W. TATE AGED 70 YEARS, 1 MONTH AND 19 DAYS		FEB. 1, 1919	
89	MARY TATE WIFE OF GEORGE W. TATE AGED 70 YEARS AND 18 DAYS		APRIL 8, 1915	
90	CORPL. S. P. SHOWALTERS CO. H 12TH PA CAV. CIVIL WAR			
91	FLORA TATE DAU. OF G. W. AND S. R. TATE AGED 12 YEARS, 6 MONTHS AND 22 DAYS		APRIL 13, 1888	
92	WILLIAM F. TATE SON OF G. W. AND S. R. TATE AGED 8 YEARS, 11 MONTHS AND 17 DAYS		MAR. 17, 1888	
93	BESSIE M. TATE DAU. OF G. W. AND M. TATE AGED 1 YEAR, 11 MONTHS AND 23 DAYS		JAN. 30, 1888	
94	_____________ PITTMAN			THIS STONE IS BROKEN AND MOSTLY UNREADABLE. ONLY A PIECE IS LEFT.
95	HARVEY SIMMONS SON OF T AND E. SIMMONS AGED 1 YEAR, 3 MONTHS AND 8 DAYS		AUG. 3, 1884	
96	THOMAS SIMMONS CIVIL WAR	JAN. 31, 1847	JAN. 14, 1929	DOUBLE STONE
97	ELIZABETH DENEEN SIMMONS WIFE OF THOMAS SIMMONS	MAY 20, 1847	MAR. 12, 1919	
98	RUBEN J. SIMMONS	FEB. 8, 1888	JAN. 9, 1946	
99	SAMUEL H. RILEY	MAR. 22, 1853	NOV. 14, 1914	
100	CLARA RILEY	SEPT. 5, 1868	AUG. 3, 1937	QUADRUPLE STONE
101	RUBEN BRALLIER	SEPT. 22, 1863	DEC. 31, 1898	
102	INFANT DAUGHTER OF R. AND C. BRALLIER		DEC. 18, 1898	

NUMBER	NAMES/INSCRIPTIONS	BIRTH DATE	DEATH DATE	MISC. INFO.
103	NORMAN GLEN BRALLIER PRIVATE 1ST CLASS WORLD WAR I	1891	1946	
104	SAMUEL SIPES AGED 73 YEARS AND 21 DAYS		SEPT. 5, 1903	
105	MARGARET E. SIMMONS DAU. OF J. T. AND G. N. SIMMONS	AUG. 12, 1905	DEC. 7, 1905	
106	JOHN T. SIMMONS	1881	1962	DOUBLE STONE
107	GERTRUDE N. SIMMONS	1884	1964	
108	EDITH M. SIMMONS DAU. OF G. N. AND J. SIMMONS		MAY 21, 1901	
109	RUBEN T. SIMMONS SON OF G. N. AND J. SIMMONS	MAR. 8, 1900	JULY 13, 1900	
110	ALFRED T. SIMMONS AGED 32 YEARS, 1 MONTH AND 20 DAYS		FEB. 20, 1897	
111	BERTHA GRUBB		1888	
112	SARAH SIMMONS AGED 72 YEARS, 9 MONTHS AND 28 DAYS		MAY 2, 1891	DOUBLE STONE
113	AARON SIMMONS AGED 89 YEARS, 7 MONTHS AND 11 DAYS		DEC. 7, 1903	
114	ELIZA A. SIMMONS AGED 54 YEARS, 7 MONTHS AND 16 DAYS		APRIL 28, 1897	
115	WILLIAM SIMMONS AGED 66 YEARS, 3 MONTHS AND 20 DAYS CIVIL WAR		NOV. 17, 1904	
116	BARBARA SIMMONS WIFE OF WILLIAM SIMMONS AGED 67 YEARS AND 23 DAYS		JAN. 19, 1921	
117	URIAH SPARKS AGED 50 YEARS, 10 MONTHS AND 6 DAYS CO. H 107TH REGT. PA VOL. CIVIL WAR		MAR. 13, 1893	
118	HANNAH SHAFFER AGED ABOUT 58 YEARS		OCT. 15, 1856	
119	ABRAHAM SHAFFER CO. K. 133RD REGT. P. V. I. CO. G. 186TH REGT. P. V. I. AGED ABOUT 86 YEARS		APRIL 15, 1916	

NUMBER	NAMES/INSCRIPTIONS	BIRTH DATE	DEATH DATE	MISC. INFO.
120	VERNON CARL SHAFFER AGED 28 YEARS, 7 MONTHS AND 12 DAYS		MAY 23, 1907	
121	BEATRICE HAZEL SHAFFER DAU. OF V. AND M. SHAFFER	JULY 30, 1901	FEB. 14, 1919	
122	HATTIE BLANCHE SHAFFER DAU. OF A. AND S. SHAFFER AGED 6 YEARS, 5 MONTHS AND 27 DAYS		DEC. 12, 1887	
123	GRANT Y. SHAFFER SON OF A. AND S. SHAFFER AGED 3 YEARS, 1 MONTH AND 10 DAYS		OCT. 25, 1887	
124	JAMES HAROLD SHAFFER AGED 1 YEAR, 2 MONTHS AND 11 DAYS		FEB. 20, 1885	
125	SUE SLEIGHTER SMITH	FEB. 11, 1868	OCT. 8, 1946	
126	S. ELLA MILLER	AUG. 20, 1872	MAY 28, 1925	DOUBLE STONE
127	DAVID L. MILLER	MAR. 5, 1865	SEPT. 11, 1945	
128	LLOYD R. MILLER SON OF D. AND E. MILLER		MAR. 19, 1912	
129	HOWARD P. COLLEDGE SON OF J. AND A. S. COLLEDGE AGED 5 YEARS, 4 MONTHS AND 21 DAYS		AUG. 8, 1902	
130	IDA MAY BULLOCK	AUG. 27, 1897	JULY 15, 1973	
131	ABRAHAM MARTIN AGED 63 YEARS		MAR. 17, 1834	
132	ELIZA MARTIN WIFE OF ABRAHAM MARTIN AGED 47 YEARS		DEC. 27, 1817	
133	WILLIAM MARTIN AGED 23 YEARS		AUG. 14, 1836	

Cemetery List (Section 2)

NUMBER	NAMES/INSCRIPTIONS	BIRTH DATE	DEATH DATE	MISC. INFO.
THE FOLLOWING GRAVES ARE A SEPARATE SECTION LOCATED IN THE UPPER PART OF THIS CEMETERY. THANK YOU TO RON MCFARLAND WHO PROVIDED ME WITH THE INFORMATION FOR THIS SECTION.				
134	ALBERT H. SHOWALTER	JAN. 14, 1878	APRIL 10, 1951	
135	JOHN W. GARLICK	MAR. 3, 1859	FEB. 5, 1898	
136	RUSSEL A. GARLICK	1888	1899	
137	DONALD E. FLUKE	SEPT. 3, 1953	SEPT. 11, 2004	ALSO INSCRIBED ON STONE SPECIAL FRIEND EUGENE G. LAZAR
138	LYDIA E. FLUKE	FEB. 28, 1915	SEPT. 2, 1984	DOUBLE STONE
139	JOHN H. FLUKE	DEC. 7, 1914	DEC. 11, 2008	
140	FLORENCE M. DIEHL	MAR. 5, 1913	JAN. 30, 2010	DOUBLE STONE
141	WARREN E. DIEHL	JULY 10, 1913	SEPT. 30, 2000	
142	WILLIAM H. R. SMITH SON OF STEPHEN AND LAVINA SMITH	1943	1959	DOUBLE STONE
143	PHYLLIS J. SMITH DAU. OF STEPHEN AND LAVINA SMITH	1929	1947	
144	LAVINA E. SMITH	1908	1990	DOUBLE STONE
145	STEPHEN S. SMITH	1906	1974	
146	ARLENE P. SHOMO	1937	2004	FUNERAL HOME MARKER FROM GEISEL FUNERAL HOME
147	MARY ALICE SPARKS	NOV. 12, 1929	MAR. 28, 1981	DOUBLE STONE
148	VERNON J. SPARKS	JULY 29, 1914	JAN. 27, 1982	
149	ROBIN LEE SPARKS SON OF VERNON J. AND MARYALICE SPARKS	MAY 5, 1961	SEPT. 27, 1978	
150	JAMES C. SPARKS	1951	1955	
151	WILLIAM D. C. SPARKS	1902	1973	DOUBLE STONE
152	NELLIE O. E. SPARKS	1911	1989	
153	VIRGINIA O. M. MARLIN	MAY 6, 1929	MAR. 13, 1999	
154	SMALL STONE NO INSCRIPTION			
155	SMALL STONE NO INSCRIPTION			
156	SMALL STONE INSCRIBED M. F.			
157	EDNA N. MARLIN	JULY 17, 1956	MAY 26, 2015	

NUMBER	NAMES/INSCRIPTIONS	BIRTH DATE	DEATH DATE	MISC. INFO.
158	J. ANDREW BRALLIER	OCT. 25, 1912	JULY 18, 1990	DOUBLE STONE
159	ERMA L. BRALLIER	MAR. 2, 1915	OCT. 7, 1992	
160	JOYCE ELAINE BRALLIER	SEPT. 5, 1941	JULY 6, 2006	
161	GILBERT L. BRALLIER INFANT SON OF J. ANDREW AND ERMA L. BRALLIER		JUNE 16, 1934	
162	SMALL STONE NO INSCRIPTION			
163	SMALL STONE NO INSCRIPTION			
164	SMALL STONE INSCRIBED S. F.			
165	BESSIE SPARKS MOTHER OF ERMA BRALLIER	1892	1944	
166	IDA E. SPARKS	JAN. 22, 1881	JULY 25, 1967	DOUBLE STONE
167	WILLIAM SPARKS	APRIL 6, 1880	JUNE 12, 1955	
168	MIRMA JOHN H. SPARKS PENNSYLVANIA MM1 USNR WORLD WAR I AND II	APRIL 26, 1900	MAY 14, 1943	
169	JONAS SPARKS	JUNE 16, 1848	MAR. 11, 1928	DOUBLE STONE
170	ELIZABETH SPARKS	MAY 12, 1854	JULY 15, 1918	
171	SHIRLEY MARLENE MCFARLAND DAU. OF ROY AND MILDRED MCFARLAND	NOV. 1, 1936	FEB. 21, 1938	
172	MILDRED E. MCFARLAND	1912	1968	DOUBLE STONE
173	ROY MCFARLAND	1908	1976	
174	GARY "GUS" MCFARLAND	OCT. 5, 1943	MAR. 14, 2014	NO STONE
175	CHARLIE MCFARLAND	DEC. 21, 1880	JUNE 24, 1958	DOUBLE STONE
176	EMMA M. MCFARLAND	JUNE 3, 1877	OCT. 14, 1944	
177	CHARLES MCFARLAND, JR.	FEB. 8, 1917	OCT. 17, 1979	DOUBLE STONE
178	PAULINE MCFARLAND	SEPT. 5, 1913	OCT. 7, 1998	
179	ALLEN R. MCFARLAND	JAN. 11, 1947	NOV. 23, 2005	DOUBLE STONE BROTHERS
180	RICHARD C. MCFARLAND VIETNAM	NOV. 25, 1942	AUG. 8, 2009	
181	SMALL STONE NO INSCRIPTION			
182	SMALL STONE NO INSCRIPTION			
183	INFANT MILLER SON OF L. AND A. M. MILLER	DEC. 3, 1899	DEC. 6, 1899	

NUMBER	NAMES/INSCRIPTIONS	BIRTH DATE	DEATH DATE	MISC. INFO.
184	ALICE M. MILLER AGED 29 YEARS, 6 MONTHS AND 12 DAYS	SEPT. 2, 1876	MAR. 14, 1906	
185	WORLD WAR II VETERAN NO STONE			
186	OLIVE BRALLIER	JUNE 9, 1890	NOV. 27, 1960	DOUBLE
187	WALTER LEVI BRALLIER	JUNE 21, 1888	SEPT. 23, 1957	STONE
188	JANET E. BRALLIER DAU. OF W. L. AND O. BRALLIER	JULY 19, 1933	FEB. 1, 1935	
189	CHARLES M. BRALLIER SON OF W. L. AND O. BRALLIER	SEPT. 10, 1923	OCT. 4, 1925	
190	MARY ELLEN LEADER DAU. OF D. AND K. LEADER AGED 71 YEARS AND 1 MONTH		MAR. 15, 1918	
191	MARTHA MCFARLAND	MAR. 14, 1883	DEC. 24, 1967	
192	JESSIE MCFARLAND DAU. OF A. J. AND E. MCFARLAND	SEPT. 4, 1881	JAN. 24, 1908	
193	ANDREW J. MCFARLAND CO. F. 79TH REGT. P. V. CIVIL WAR	DEC. 15, 1846	DEC. 13, 1906	DOUBLE STONE
194	ELIZABETH LEADER MCFARLAND	JAN. 12, 1850	OCT. 21, 1924	
195	GEORGE ROBERT MCFARLAND SON OF A. J. AND E. MCFARLAND	DEC. 3, 1878	NOV. 21, 1888	
196	SAMUEL FRENCH CO. K 208TH REGT. PA VOL. AGED 54 YEARS, 2 MONTHS AND 23 DAYS		OCT. 25, 1888	DOUBLE STONE
197	CATHERINE MCFARLAND FRENCH WIFE OF SAMUEL FRENCH AGED 89 YEARS, 6 MONTHS AND 11 DAYS	MAR. 21, 1835	SEPT. 21, 1924	
198	BESSIE C. FRENCH DAU. OF J. S. AND F. FRENCH	JUNE 10, 1894	JUNE 18, 1895	
199	HAROLD MCFARLAND, JR.		1952	
200	ORA MAIE MCFARLAND	DEC. 18, 1917	FEB. 27, 2002	DOUBLE
201	HAROLD MCFARLAND, SR.	SEPT. 15, 1910	FEB. 16, 1996	STONE
202	GARY P. WHITFIELD	NOB. 3, 1942		DOUBLE
203	WANDA J. WHITFIELD	JUNE 25, 1943	JULY 27, 2013	STONE

NUMBER	NAMES/INSCRIPTIONS	BIRTH DATE	DEATH DATE	MISC. INFO.
204	JAMES W. IRONS SON OF W. B. AND A. IRONS	MAY 16, 1908	OCT. 8, 1910	
205	MARY FRENCH DAU. OF STEPHEN FRECH	SEPT. 24, 1836	JAN. 14, 1911	
206	EMMA C. MCFARLAND	1872	1950	DOUBLE STONE
207	JAMES H. MCFARLAND	1867	1938	
208	SARAH ELSETTA MCFARLAND	JUNE 18, 1891	OCT. 17, 1949	
209	CORP. DANIEL W. MCFARLAND HQ. DET. PMGD. WORLD WAR I	OCT. 6, 1895	AUG. 24, 1955	
210	WILLIAM H. MCFARLAND CO. M 36TH REGT. WORLD WAR I	APRIL 4, 1893	APRIL 26, 1961	
211	WINONA M. LITTLE WIFE OF CHARLES E. LITTLE	JULY 17, 1905	AUG. 4, 1971	
212	IRENE MCKINNEY	SEPT. 27, 1899	DEC. 19, 1984	
213	ALICE W. CRAGAN	JULY 27, 1924	JAN. 31, 1928	
214	DANIEL D. MCFARLAND, SR. CPL US ARMY WORLD WAR II	OCT. 6, 1922	FEB. 7, 1996	
215	JOHN W. MCFARLAND, JR.	AUG. 13, 1927	MAY 26, 2007	
216	LOLA JOAN MCFARLAND	FEB. 3, 1935	MAR. 2, 1935	
217	NELLIE J. MCFARLAND	MAR. 24, 1895	JUNE 27, 1990	DOUBLE STONE
218	JOHN W. MCFARLAND PVT WEST VIRGINIA INFANTRY SPANISH AMERICAN WAR	MAR. 23, 1874	APRIL 14, 1952	
219	RICKY L. CRAGAN, SR.	NOV. 5, 1958	MAY 7, 2004	DOUBLE STONE
220	THERESA R. CRAGAN	FEB. 5, 1959		
221	ALMA R. CRAGAN	AUG. 16, 1926	JAN. 27, 2007	DOUBLE STONE
222	JOHN ALFRED CRAGAN US ARMY WORLD WAR II	FEB. 1, 1927	AUG. 16, 2003	
223	TERRY L. "CHIP" STEELE, JR.	JAN. 21, 1975	JAN. 23, 1999	
224	JAMES H. CRAGAN PVT US ARMY KOREA	MAR. 23, 1928	MAR. 4, 1989	
225	TERRY L. STEELE	SEPT. 24, 1950	JUNE 25, 2010	
226	SARAH C. MCFARLAND AGED 2 YEARS, 1 MONTH AND 17 DAYS		DEC. 28, 1882	
227	GERTHA V. GATES DAU. OF D. E. AND E. L. GATES	SEPT. 9, 1901	NOV. 23, 1901	UNMARKED GRAVE

NUMBER	NAMES/INSCRIPTIONS	BIRTH DATE	DEATH DATE	MISC. INFO.
228	MINNIE MAY MCFARLAND DAU. OF J. AND S. MCFARLAND AGED 6 YEARS, 10 MONTHS AND 22 DAYS		MAY 9, 1895	
229	ARDATH O. GATES DAU. OF D. E. AND E. L. GATES	MAY 10, 1903	JAN. 31, 1908	UNMARKED GRAVE
230	VIVIAN GATES DAU. OF D. E. AND E. L. GATES	JUNE 16, 1905	FEB. 1, 1908	UNMARKED GRAVE
231	JOSEPH MCFARLAND CO. F. 8TH REGT. P. R. V. C. CIVIL WAR	JULY 30, 1840	NOV. 14, 1908	DOUBLE STONE
232	SARAH RITCHEY	MAR. 3, 1847	SEPT. 16, 1925	
233	MARY S. MCFARLAND AGED 45 YEARS, 5 MONTHS AND 21 DAYS		DEC. 14, 1917	
234	DELLA RITCHEY MCFARLAND WIFE OF JAMES MCFARLAND	OCT. 28, 1884	SEPT. 29, 1907	
235	JAMES J. MCFARLAND SON OF J. AND S. MCFARLAND	DEC. 25, 1867	DEC. 25, 1905	
236	INFANT MCFARLAND SON OF J. W. AND F. MCFARLAND		JUNE 11, 1910	
237	JOHN W. MCFARLAND	DEC. 9, 1880	MAR. 26, 1925	
238	MYRTLE A. MCFARLAND	1879	1916	DOUBLE STONE
239	ROBERT. H. H. MCFARLAND	1878	1957	
240	MEARL MCFARLAND SON OF R. H. MCFARLAND		1903	
241	HENRY MCFARLAND SON OF R. H. MCFARLAND		1908	
242	MARY J. MCFARLAND HOWSARE WIFE OF SIMON HOWSARE AGED 43 YEARS, 6 MONTHS AND 28 DAYS		MAR. 1, 1896	
243	JESSE MCFARLAND		1899	
244	GEORGE V. MCFARLAND	1858	1942	

Cemetery List (Section 3)

NUMBER	NAMES/INSCRIPTIONS	BIRTH DATE	DEATH DATE	MISC. INFO.
245	IRENE GLADYS SANDS	MAY 11, 1946	SEPT. 12, 2017	
246	MARIE B. MILLIN	1922		DOUBLE STONE
247	GUY M. MILLIN	1910	1984	
248	DAVID A. CRAWFORD	1954		DOUBLE STONE
249	RICHARD M. CRAWFORD WORLD WAR II	1924	1988	
250	JOHN W. SMOKE, JR.	MAR. 24, 1949	FEB. 19, 2012	

NOTES

NOTES

NOTES

Williams Farm Cemetery

Documented: Summer of 2017

This cemetery is located on private property. Please ask permission from landowner prior to entering.

GPS Coordinates

39.980994, -78.303560

Address

McDaniel Road

Everett, PA 15537

Cemetery List

NUMBER	NAMES/INSCRIPTIONS	BIRTH DATE	DEATH DATE	MISC. INFO.
1	BERNADOTTE A. WILLIAMS SON OF ASA & L. A. WILLIAMS AGED 24 YEARS, 2 MONTHS AND 9 DAYS		SEPT. 11, 1871	STONE IS BROKEN AND WORN
2	ISAAC W. WILLIAMS SON OF ASA & L. A. WILLIAMS		JAN. 25, 1858	STONE IS WORN. MOSTLY UNREADABLE
3	LUCRETIA WILLIAMS DAU. OF ASA & L. A. WILLIAMS AGED 1 YEAR, 7 MONTHS AND 11 DAYS		JAN. 2, 1858	
4	VICTORINA WILLIAMS DAU. OF ASA & L. A. WILLIAMS AGED 6 YEARS, 1 MONTH AND 18 DAYS		JAN. 29, 1858	
5	HENRY L. E. WILLIAMS SON OF ASA AND L. A. WILLIAMS AGED 11 YEARS, 1 MONTH AND 13 DAYS		JAN. 31, 1859	
6	EMMA WILLIAMS DAU. OF ASA & L. A. WILLIAMS AGED 20 YEARS, 5 MONTHS AND 22 DAYS		AUG. 8, 1864	STONE IS BROKEN
7	LUCRETIA AKERS WILLIAMS WIFE OF ASA WILLIAMS AGED 77 YEARS, 2 MONTHS AND 24 DAYS		JAN. 1, 1893	
8	ASA WILLIAMS AGED 74 YEARS, 4 MONTHS AND 17 DAYS		MAR. 10, 1884	
9	MATILDA WILLIAMS DAU. OF W. & S. WILLIAMS AGED 21 YEARS AND 10 MONTHS		AUG. 30, 1861	
10	WILLIAM WILLIAMS AGED 67 YEARS, 11 MONTHS AND 23 DAYS		SEPT. 22, 1875	

NUMBER	NAMES/INSCRIPTIONS	BIRTH DATE	DEATH DATE	MISC. INFO.
11	SARAH WILLIAMS WIFE OF WILLIAM WILLIAMS AGED 41 YEARS, 6 MONTHS AND 19 DAYS		MARCH 1, 1851	
12	RANDOLPH WILLIAMS SON OF WILLIAM AND SARAH WILLIAMS AGED 7 YEARS, 3 MONTHS AND 24 DAYS		DEC. 26, 1855	
13	JANE WILLIAMS WIFE OF WILLIAM WILLIAMS AGED 57 YEARS, 11 MONTHS AND 15 DAYS		OCT. 26, 1857	
14	MARGARET WINTER WIFE OF JOSEPH WINTER		NOV. 24, 1861	IT APPEARS THIS STONE WAS BROKEN AND THEN REATTACHED
15	SARAH M. WINTER DAU. OF J. & M. WINTER AGED 3 MONTHS AND 17 DAYS		MAR. 1, 1862	
16	JULIA MENCH WIFE OF G. W. MENCH AGED 75 YEARS, 6 MONTHS AND 19 DAYS		JULY 11, 1877	
17	JONAS WILLIAMS AGED 34 YEARS, 1 MONTH AND 21 DAYS	OCT. 28, 1805	DEC. 19, 1839	
18	SOLOMON WILLIAMS AGED 43 YEARS, 4 MONTHS AND 8 DAYS	MARCH 4, 1770	JULY 12, 1813	
19	MARY WILLIAMS AGED 67 YEARS, 3 MONTHS AND 11 DAYS	SEPT. 1, 1766	DEC. 12, 1833	
20	JOHN WILLIAMS AGED 79 YEARS REVOLUTIONARY WAR		MAY 21, 1809	
21	CYRUS WILLIAMS SON OF JEDUTHUN & MARY WILLIAMS AGED 8 MONTHS		AUG. 13, 1833	
22	SOLOMON C. WILLIAMS SON OF JEDUTHUN AND MARY WILLIAMS AGED 1 YEAR, 11 MONTHS AND 2 DAYS		APRIL 18, 1840	

NUMBER	NAMES/INSCRIPTIONS	BIRTH DATE	DEATH DATE	MISC. INFO.
23	JEDUTHUN WILLIAMS AGED 80 YEARS, 3 MONTHS AND 9 DAYS		AUG. 6, 1879	
24	MARY WILLIAMS WIFE OF JEDUTHUN WILLIAMS AGED 71 YEARS, 8 MONTHS AND 21 DAYS		JULY 9, 1875	
25	HANNAH ESHELMAN WIFE OF JOHN ESHELMAN AGED 25 YEARS, 3 MONTHS AND 12 DAYS		NOV. 17, 1856	
26	SAMUEL WILLIAMS AGED 47 YEARS, 9 MONTHS AND 29 DAYS	JAN. 8, 1795	NOV. 6, 1842	
27	CATHARINE WILLIAMS AGED 35 YEARS, 2 MONTHS AND 17 DAYS		NOV. 17, 1838	
28	SARAH ELLEN WILLIAMS AGED 2 YEARS, 1 MONTH AND 27 DAYS	SEPT. 4, 1837	NOV. 1, 1839	
29	LEWIS C. MCDANIEL SON OF W. & C. M. MCDANIEL AGED 2 MONTHS AND 1 DAY		MAR. 4, 1865	
30	CATHARINE M. MCDANIEL WIFE OF WILSON MCDANIEL AGED 29 YEARS, 11 MONTHS AND 20 DAYS		NOV. 7, 1868	

Unnamed Church Cemetery

An unnamed church cemetery is located off of West Graceville Road where a German Baptist Brethren Church used to sit. According to a book entitled: "A History of the Church of the Brethren in the Middle District of Pennsylvania" (Prepared and Published Under the Supervision of the District Conference through its Home Mission Board, Introduction is Dated 1924) Jacob Burket donated land for the church which was built in 1887 and a burial ground was later added. The following is quoted directly from the book:

"Ground being donated by Jacob Burket, the Fairview house, five miles east from Everett, was erected in 1887 at a cost of about $500.00. Building committee: William Simmons, Jacob Burket and David S. Clapper. Dedication day was so stormy that no special service was held. At this place services at stated intervals have been held ever since, though the congregation has not increased in numbers very greatly."

Following is a copy of the Deed from Jacob Burket to the German Baptist Brethren Church, dated August 1892. The land consisting of 60 perches was transferred after the church was built in 1887.

in the township of East Providence in the County of Bedford and State of Pennsylvania, beginning at a post at the Public Road, thence through the said Burket's land North seventy six and three fourths degrees [illegible] eight rods to a post, thence North thirteen and three fourths degree East ten rods to a post, [illegible] six and three fourths degree East eight and nine tenths rods, and South [illegible] ten degrees West, [illegible] tenth rods to the place of beginning. Containing sixty square perches, being part of the Real Estate, [illegible] was of Daniel Ritchey late of said township and County deceased, and Samuel Ritchey Executor of last will and testament of said deceased conveyed the same to the parties of the first part herein.

Together with all and singular the improvements, ways, waters, water courses, rights, liberties, privileges, hereditaments and appurtenances whatsoever thereunto belonging or in anywise appertaining, and the reversions and remainders, rents, issues and profits thereof; and all the estate, right, title, interest property, claim and demand whatsoever of the said part of the first part, in law equity or otherwise, howsoever of in and to the same and every part thereof.

To have and to hold the said lot of sixty square perches of land for church purposes only, the hereditament and premises hereby granted, or mentioned and intended so to be, with the appurtenances, unto the said parties of the second part, & their successors in office, to and for the only proper use and behoof of the said parties of the second part & their successors in office, forever.

And Jacob Burket and Pheba his wife, David Burket and Ida his wife, the said parties of the first part, for themselves and their successors in office, do by these presents, covenant, [illegible] and agree to and with the said parties of the second part, their successors in office, that they the said parties of the first part, their heirs, all and singular the hereditaments and premises herein above described and granted, or mentioned and intended so to be, with the appurtenances, unto the said parties of the second part their successors in office, against them the said parties of the first part, and their heirs, and against all and every other person or persons whomsoever, lawfully claiming or to claim the same or any part thereof, shall and will warrant and forever defend.

In Witness Whereof, The said parties of the first part have to these presents set their hands and seals, Date the day and year first above written. Signed, sealed and   Jacob Burket [Seal]   David Burket [Seal] delivered in the presence of us: E. C. Wearrling   Pheba ^{her mark} Burket [Seal]   Ida M. Burket [Seal]
       G. W. Richey

Received the day of the date of the above Indenture, of the above named Elders in trust the sum of one dollar, lawful money of the United States, being the consideration money above mentioned in full

Witness: C. C. Wearrling   Jacob Burket
       G. W. Richey   David Burket

Commonwealth of Pennsylvania
    Bedford County } ss.   On this 4th day of August A.D. 1892 before me, the subscriber a Justice of the Peace in and for said County, personally came the above named Jacob Burket & Pheba his wife, David Burket and Ida his wife, [illegible]

After the Church closed, the Trustees deeded the Church and Cemetery to George McGraw. The deed for that follows. A Cemetery Lot with dimensions of 40 feet by 50 feet is mentioned in this Deed. Although there is no documentation of who may be buried in this cemetery and no trace of it today, it did exist according to this deed and to some who remember seeing it in passing by. Please note the Everett Brethren Church which is mentioned in the deed below was formerly known as the German Baptist Brethren Church. The church was eventually torn down and the exact location of the church and cemetery is not known and no stones remain in existence today.

61521

Deed
Everett Brethren Church
by Trustees
To
George McGraw
Dated January 26, 1933
Parcel—East Providence Twp
Consideration $25.00

Everett, Bedford Co., Penna.
Baptist Brethren Church.

This Indenture Made the
Twenty Sixth day of January
in the year of our Lord
one thousand nine hundred
and Thirty Three
Between Francis Baker,
D. C. Cypher, and W. B.
Dilling, Trustees of the
Everett Brethren Church,
Formerly known as German
Baptist Brethren Church, Hopewell Congregation,

Parties of the first Part, and George McGraw of East Providence Township, Bedford Co., Penna., of the second part.

Witnesseth, That the said part of the first part, for and in consideration of the sum of Twenty five Dollars, lawful money of the United States of America, unto us was well and truly paid by the said part of the second part, at or before the sealing and delivery of these presents, the receipt whereof is hereby acknowledged, have granted, bargained, sold, aliened, enfeoffed, released, conveyed and confirmed, and by these presents do grant, bargain, sell, alien, enfeoff, release, convey and confirm unto the said part of the second part, George McGraw and his heirs and assigns.

All the following described Real Estate situated in the Township of East Providence in the County of Bedford and State of Pennsylvania. Beginning at a post at the Public Road. Thence through the land of Jacob Burket and Phebe his wife, and David Burket and Ida his wife. North Seventy Six and three fourths degrees west eight Rods to a Post. Thence North thirteen and three fourths degrees east ten Rods to a Post. South Seventy Six and three fourths degrees east eight and nine tenths Rods and South nineteen degrees West ten and one tenth Rods to the place of Beginning. Containing Sixty Square Perches with the following Exceptions. A Cemetary Lot Located in the North West corner of said plat, with dimentions of Fourty feet east and west and Fifty feet north and South and Right of Way to same.

The above plat being part of the Real Estate which was of Daniel Ritchey late of said Township and County, Deceased, and Samuel Ritchey, Executor of the last will and Testament of said Deceased, Conveyed the same to Jacob Burket and Phebe his wife, Daniel Burket and Ida his wife of West Providence Township, Bedford County, and State of Pennsylvania. Who conveyed same to Henry Clapper and David Clapper Elders in Trust for the German Baptists Church of the Brethren, Hopewell Congregation and their successors in Office. Who are Trustees of the Everett Brethren Church which was formerly called German Baptists Brethren Church of Hopewell Congregation. Parties of the first part Deeds. Their Deed having been Recorded in Recorders Office of Bedford County Pennsylvania on October Twenty fifth Eighteen Hundred ninety three in Deed Book, Vol 52 Page 150 &c.

Together with all and singular the improvements ways waters water courses rights liberties privileges hereditaments and appurtenances whatsoever thereunto

belonging or in anywise appertaining, and the reversions and
remainders, rents, issues and profits thereof; and all the
estate, right, title, interest, property, claim and demand whatsoever of the said parties of the first part, in law, equity, or
otherwise, howsoever, of, in and to the same; and every part
thereof.

To Have and to Hold the said lot of sixty perches of
land less the Exceptions as first above mentioned hereditaments and premises hereby granted, or mentioned and intended to be, with the appurtenances, unto the said party of the
second part, his heirs and assigns, to and for the only
proper use and behoof of the said part of the second
part his heirs and assigns forever. And Francis
Baker, D. S. Gepher and W. B. Dilling, Trustees of the
Church of the Brethren, Everett Congregation, the said
parties of the first part, for Previous Officers their
executors and administrators, do by these presents
covenant, grant and agree to and with the said
parts of the second part, his heirs and assigns that
they the said parties of the first part Previous Officers
heirs, all and singular the hereditaments and premises herein above described and granted, or mentioned
and intended so to be, with the appurtenances, unto the
said party of the second part, his heirs and assigns,
against them the said parties of the first part and
Previous Officers heirs, and against all and every other person
or persons whomsoever, lawfully claiming or to claim the
same or any part thereof, shall and will warrant and
forever defend.

In Witness Whereof, the said parties of the first part do
to these presents set our hand and seal. Dated the
day and year first above written.

Signed, Sealed and Delivered
in the presence of us   Francis Baker   (Seal)
    D. B. Kagarise   D. C. Cypher   (Seal)
    Fred L. Hershberger   W. B. Dilling   (Seal)

Received the day of the date of the above named Trustees
the sum of Twenty Five Dollars lawful money of the
United States. Being the consideration money above
mentioned in full.
Witness:
                              W. B. Dilling   Sec. Treas.
State of Pennsylvania. }
Bedford County.   } ss.
        On this 26th day of January A.D. 1933, before me
the subscriber, a notary public personally came
the above named Francis Baker, D. C. Cypher and
W. B. Dilling who in due form of law acknowledged the foregoing
Indenture to be their act and deed, desiring the same to be
recorded as such.
        Witness my hand and official seal the day and year aforesaid.
                        Fred L. Hershberger   N.P. (Seal)
                                Notary Public
        Commission Expires March 2, 1933.

        Recorded and Compared February 14, 1938.
                        Clarence A. J. Diehl.
                                Recorder.

Unnamed Farm Cemetery #1

A cemetery is located on the Barkman Farm off of Milk and Water Road, Everett, PA. Some of the people that are buried in this cemetery are supposedly from a Morris family. When discovered there were no inscribed stones visible in this cemetery, only unmarked field stones. A photo of the cemetery is unavailable as there is nothing left of the cemetery today. Thanks to Angie Price for providing this information.

Unnamed Farm Cemetery #2

A cemetery is located on the McGraw Farm just off of West Graceville Road, Everett, PA. According to Delores Cogan, who provided me with information, some of the graves located here were moved to a Church Cemetery nearby with the exception of a grave belonging to a male by the last name of French and two others belonging to children. The exact location of this cemetery is not known and no stones remain in existence.

NOTES

NOTES

NOTES

NOTES

NOTES

# NOTES

NOTES

C

D

H

I

J

K

Y

Z